WHEN OFFENSE KNOCKS

WHEN OFFENSE KNOCKS

GET OFFENDED LESS, TO CHANGE THE WORLD MORE

ROB SHEPHERD

XULON ELITE

Xulon Press Elite
2301 Lucien Way #415
Maitland, FL 32751
407.339.4217
www.xulonpress.com

Unless otherwise indicated, Scripture quotations taken from the
Holy Bible, New International Version (NIV). Copyright © 1973,
1978, 1984, 2011 by Biblica, Inc.™. Used by permission. All rights
reserved.

Paperback ISBN-13: 978-1-66287-021-7
Ebook ISBN-13: 978-1-66287-022-4

This book is dedicated to, Monica, Hayden, and Reese.

I love you with all my heart! This book is birthed out of the many things we try to practice as a family including, "Treat others like you want to be treated." You three are my favorite!

Thank you for purchasing *When Offense Knocks!*
All of the author's proceeds from this book
will be given to needy children. His own.
Thank you for helping to pay for their braces,
and future college!

PRAISE FOR *WHEN OFFENSE KNOCKS*

Rob totally nails it here: "Life change doesn't happen by simply gathering information. It happens when individuals apply what they learn."

Exactly. And this book is about doing the actual stuff Jesus said to do. Forgiving is hard, yes, but a life of unforgiveness is way harder. So thankful for Rob's addition to this incredibly important topic!

—Brant Hansen,
Author of *Unoffendable* and *The Men We Need*

Offense isn't hard to come by these days. But when we look a little past the surface, we'll begin to see people who God loves and cherishes. We all get offended from time to time, but our perspective and how we respond can change the game. Rob's' message in *When Offense Knocks* is a must read!

- Dino Rizzo
Executive Director, ARC (Association of Related Churches)

People continually talk about how easily offended everyone is but few people are sharing what to do about it. Rob's book will inspire, make you laugh, and challenge you to respond like Jesus when you are offended.

- Chris Sonksen
CEO and Founder of ChurchBOOM, author of *Saving Your Church from Itself*, *When Your Church Feels Stuck*, and *Quit Church*.

Everyone is offended, but what good does it do us? That's the question that my friend, Rob Shepherd, is asking in "When Offense Knocks." In his new book, you will be inspired and challenged to love the people that offend you the most.

- Clayton King
Founder/President of Clayton King Ministries, Teaching Pastor, author, and evangelist

In today's time, it's much easier to pick a side than to pull up a chair. People would rather throw opinions back and forth not realizing the damage it causes to one another and relationships as a whole. Because of our climate, we can find ourselves caught up in this culture and being offended because of it. Rob offers some incredible principles and practicals for how we can move from being offended to making a difference the way God intended.

- Edwin Jones
Pastor of The Bridge Church

I met Rob years ago through the world of blogging. From there I have seen how he handles the internet with grace and truth. I'm excited for you to read his new book, "When Offense Knocks" because I believe you will learn how to do that in your life!

- John Finkelde
Coach and Consultant at Grow A Healthy Church

I love the scripture verse, a quiet answer turns away wrath. I deeply feel that we need more quiet answers in our culture. We all get offended, however I wonder what would happen if we got offended less. Just maybe we would solve our problems rather than shouting at one another. Great job Rob, in helping mend the divide in our world.

- Maina Mwaura
Journalist, and freelance writer who has interviewed over 500 influential leaders, including two US Presidents, and three Vice-Presidents. He is also the author of The Influential Mentor.

TABLE OF CONTENTS

INTRODUCTION

Offense is everywhere. It seems like everyone is offended by everything. According to one national poll, 94% of Republicans, 82% of Independents, and 70% of Democrats agree that people are too easily offended.[1] It doesn't seem like we can get Americans to agree on much of anything, but 81% of Americans agree that people are too easily offended! At that rate, a politician should adopt the campaign slogan, "We are all offended!" He or she would win because the only thing we are united on is that we are all offended.

I keep reading about how everyone is offended by everything, but yet I find very few people offering solutions. Something has to change, and I believe it can change with you! Simply telling someone they are too easily offended is as effective as telling an irate spouse to "Calm down." Saying "Calm down" when your spouse is irate feels like a good idea in the moment. Unfortunately, it doesn't get the results one hopes to achieve. It doesn't work! Yet, people continue to do it. So, when it comes to offense, it seems like a lot of people understand it's annoying and unproductive, but don't know that there are other options.

---

[1] https://morningconsult.com/2019/04/24/pc-and-prejudice-gauging-divides-in-americas-culture-war/

I wrote this book because I desperately want Christians to make a difference. I believe being offended gets in the way of making a difference. Being offended takes energy. All of us have limited energy, so what if we could free up some energy by not getting offended so easily and put that energy towards making a practical difference in the world? In other words, let's get offended less to change the world more.

This book is divided into four sections. The first section's goal is to clearly define why Christians should respond differently to offense. It's the "Why" behind what I believe. The following three sections are practical ways Christians can work on making a difference in place of being offended. It's the "What" of the book. Specifically, it's what to do in order to be offended less. As a Christian, I want to represent Jesus in everything I do and that includes my responses to those who trigger me. I want the same for you. In the end, I am presenting a healthy way to deal with offenses. It's a way that can bring a healthy change. I believe you can be part of the solution to changing the world when you get triggered. In order to do that, you will have to do your part.

You see, life change doesn't happen by simply gathering information. It happens when individuals apply what they learn. Learning is an active process. People learn by doing. So here are three quick ways to get the most out of this book.

THREE WAYS TO GET THE MOST OUT OF THIS BOOK

1. Read with a pen or highlighter. Underline phrases or ideas that challenge you. Revisit what you have high lighted on a regular basis to help remind you of what you want to do.

2. Read this book with a group. This is a good book to read alone, but it will be even better when you read it with someone. Invite a friend to read this with you. Read it as a small group at church, or with a book club. Reading with a group invites accountability to finish reading the book (How many times have you started a book but have not finished it?). Group reading also allows time for discussion. It's in the discussion of the ideas presented in this book that I believe most life changes will happen.

3. Take notes on what you are going to do. Almost every book comes with some blank pages at the beginning or the end of the book. Use these to jot down some big takeaways.

Alright, now that we have covered some basics, let's jump into chapter 1!

CHAPTER 1

ANOTHER OPTION

"Don't leave. Don't abandon. Engage."
—Jon Stewart

I often hear people share how everyone is offended by every-thing these days. Because of social media, we may be more exposed to what offends others, but I don't think it's a new thing. I grew up in the glorious 1980s. To this day, I feel like it's the best decade ever. It's closely followed by the 90s. Growing up in the church in the 80s felt like Christians signed up for the offense of the month club, where we became offended about something different every month. I love the 80s and think it was one of the most innovative and creative decades ever. It gave us Magic Johnson, Indiana Jones, Transformers, and Hair Metal. Pop culture was creative and breaking new ground, and the Church had a lot of thoughts about it. As a kid in church, it left a mark on me to hear adults talk about what we were going to boycott. A lot of the conversation was around enter tainment, but there were other things like restau-rants that also were boycotted be-cause they supported a movie that of-fended Christians. I distinctly remember an adult lecturing us kids about how we needed to boycott Smurfs because their name

1

means "little demon". Come to find out, that is not what the word Smurf means. What's fascinating is this church lady who felt so strongly about Smurfs did not change my opinion of them. I loved them! I watched the cartoon every Saturday, had a very robust collection of the figurines, and even had the entire Smurf village play set. I remember being told to avoid He-Man because only God has the power. I remember loving *Star Wars* and after seeing the movie the *Return of the Jedi*, I had to defend why the "force" was not a demonic power. I was five—as in five years old. I'm not sure what logic I used to defend my point, but somehow, I won the argument because I was able to still love all things Star Wars. Growing up in the church, there was a war-like mindset. The idea was that the culture was our enemy and we needed to fight against it.

This line of thinking carried over into the 90s. At one point in the 90s, the church tried to boycott Disney. I was never really sure why we were supposed to boycott Disney, but for a few weeks I felt like I had to sneak watch movies like *Aladdin* and *Lion King*. It was like we needed to close the doors, turn off the lights, and not tell anyone we were watching Disney for movie night. Oh, and if the pastor calls, "Tell him we are watching porn". That seemed to be less offensive during this season.

I love the fact that I grew up in church! As a pastor, I still love the church. I have way more great memories from church than I do negative ones. My observations about the boycotts in the church aren't meant to be negative. It was a part of my early years of church, and it left a mark. My observation is that today's cancel culture feels a lot like growing up in church in the 80s and 90s. When I ask the question, "What good did all that offense do?" I can see very little good. It didn't stop people from enjoying those things. It didn't stop me from watching the

Smurfs. It didn't change the culture. It did not cause massive numbers of people to turn to Jesus.

What good is our offense doing? That's a question that I don't see a lot of people asking. When you get offended, you will have a reaction. Does that reaction lead people to love Jesus? Are we satisfied with simply isfied with simply being offended by something? There are a lot of offensive things in the culture today.

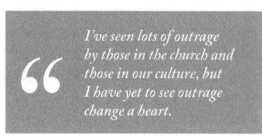

I've seen lots of outrage by those in the church and those in our culture, but I have yet to see outrage change a heart.

There are things that should bother the church. I am not proposing that we should not be offended by truly offensive things. What I am trying to do with this book is help us learn how to do something productive with our offense. If how you respond to offense doesn't lead people to love Jesus, and love other people, then you need a new strategy. When you reflect on how you respond to offense, what results do you see? I've seen lots of outrage by those in the church and those in our culture, but I have yet to see outrage change a heart.

I believe Christians need to look carefully at how we are responding to offense. I believe we need to ask the question, "What good is my offense doing?"

WHY DON'T WE ASK THAT QUESTION?

If you simply look at the results of most of our offense, you'll see that our reaction doesn't get great results. It's like the age old saying, "To do the same thing over and over again and expect different results is insane!" Yet, when it comes to our offense, we get offended without asking what good it did? I believe the reason we do that can be found in the definition of offense.

The dictionary defines offense as "to cause (a person or group) to feel <u>hurt</u>, angry, or upset by something said or done."[2]

At its core, an offense is a hurt. I wish I was so noble that I only got offended at injustices of the world. The truth is, I got offended one time because my dad asked if I wanted some slacks from JC Penney. My poor dad didn't see my wrath coming. What he didn't know was that as an insecure 14-year-old, I was desperately seeking approval from friends at school and I knew that could not be found at JC Penney. I needed jeans from the GAP, and I needed him to stop calling them slacks.

At its core, being offended is a hurt. Whenever we are hurt, we respond to the pain. We all respond to offense in different ways. For some, it's yelling. For others, it's withdrawing. Some prefer confrontation, and some prefer avoidance.

We often may not even define it as offense, but it is. When we don't get our way it's an offense. When we don't feel included it's an offense. When our feelings get hurt it is an offense. Because the offense is a hurt we often do not think about how our reaction will impact others.

We don't really spend much time thinking about how we respond to offense, but I would argue we should. What effect does our offense have on others? In the church world I often see Christians simply leave a church whenever they become offended. In their mind that is easier than dealing with the conflict. This is problematic because issues are not resolved and it leads the person or church who is left feeling abandoned. The

---

2 Merriam-Webster Dictionary

other option I see often in church circles is ranting about the issue. These rants can either be passive aggressive and made online or directly to the person in a strongly worded email or letter. I don't see a lot of value in ghosting a church by simply leaving. I also do not see a lot of positive results after a strongly worded email has been sent. The point is we often respond to offense out of hurt. When we respond to an offense, does it get the results we are seeking? These are questions I've been asking a lot.

THE OTHER OPTION

We are so busy being offended by everything that we don't take the time to ask, "What good is it doing?" If being offended doesn't change the world and make it a better place, then there has to be another option. Jesus offered that option when He said,

> "Love your enemies, do good to those who hate
> you, bless those who curse you, pray for those
> who mistreat you" (Luke 6:27- 28).

Jesus' teaching was and still is radical. Imagine responding to an offense by doing good to the person who offended you. Imagine responding to an offense by blessing the very person who offended you. Imagine responding to an offense by praying

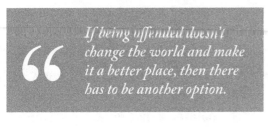

If being offended doesn't change the world and make it a better place, then there has to be another option.

for the person who hurt you. This seems impossibly difficult until we think about how we wish people responded to us when we are guilty of offense. When we offend others, we want a second chance, grace, and forgiveness. Yet, when someone offends us, we want justice. The way of Jesus pushes back against our natural desire to hurt people like we've been hurt. Instead of getting back at our enemies, we are to love

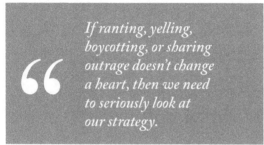

If ranting, yelling, boycotting, or sharing outrage doesn't change a heart, then we need to seriously look at our strategy.

them. Now, I know that not everyone who offends you is an enemy, but if the standard is to love your enemies, then it should apply to those who offend you.

PUSH BACK

This is where the massive push back comes. The thought is, if we don't get angry and if we don't get offended then the world won't change. This is something with which I wrestle. I ask questions like, "What about the real injustices in the world?" What about the things that are truly offensive? Shouldn't we react in anger? The answer to that question is, "No." If ranting, yelling, boycotting, or sharing outrage doesn't change a heart, then we need to seriously look at our strategy.

I'm less concerned with what offends and more concerned with what to do with that offense. When you get offended, you have a reaction to that offense. You may not even know why you react the way you do, but you will have a reaction. If offense is a hurt, then it's natural to react to pain, even when that pain is emotional. An offense is a hurt, and until that hurt is properly dealt with, the pain does not go away. So much bitterness, broken relationships, and toxicity is caused by an offense that never heals. The problem with not healing is that we end up bleeding on people who didn't offend us. An offense from our childhood can cause harm for future relationships. An

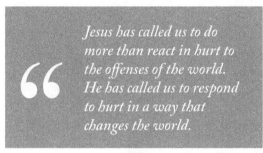

Jesus has called us to do more than react in hurt to the offenses of the world. He has called us to respond to hurt in a way that changes the world.

offense at work can cause us to react in anger to our family once we get home. An offense is a hurt. If not dealt with properly, that hurt becomes a wound. In order to heal, we need to learn how we deal with the things that offend us in a healthy way.

Imagine walking through the woods and while minding your own business you step on a bear trap. That's a horrible thought, and I truly hope it never happens to you. It's one of the many reasons I am indoorsy...fear of bear traps. Just for illustration's sake, imagine that when you step on said bear trap, you react. No one would judge you for reacting to stepping on the bear trap. However, if your reaction does more harm than good, it will make the situation worse. Imagine that in your hurt, you yank your foot out of the trap before you open the claws. That one act, as gruesome as it is, is a picture of what we do with offense. When we step on offense, we react. Offense is a hurt, so we naturally react to that pain. Our reaction can either make the situation better or worse. Because offense is a hurt, we tend to react and not ask what good it did. We react with outrage, but rarely ask if it did any good. If the point is simply to take a stand, then outrage is good enough, but I don't think that should be the point. Jesus has called us to do more than react in hurt to the offenses of the world. He has called us to respond to hurt in a way that changes the world. In order to do that we have to engage with those that offend us in a way that wins them over.

Here is a real life example that doesn't involve a gruesome bear trap. In 2022 two activists threw tomato soup on the famous Vincent van Gogh's Sunflower painting. They didn't stop there. After they tried to ruin the painting they took out glue and tried to glue their hands to the wall. Thankfully the painting wasn't damaged because there was a thin, clear piece of glass over it. The activists were

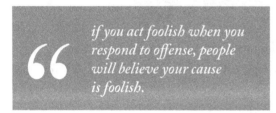

if you act foolish when you respond to offense, people will believe your cause is foolish.

offended by a cause they believed in, so they passionately responded to that offense by throwing soup on a priceless piece of art. Here's the problem, their response did not inspire anyone else to take up their cause. In fact it did the opposite. The goal of your reaction should be to get people to agree with your cause. The activists acted like spoiled chil-dren; therefore the general response is to see their cause as childish. They actually had the opposite effect on people. People were outraged by the tomato soup stunt and then dismissed their cause all together. To put it bluntly, if you act foolish when you respond to offense, people will believe your cause is foolish. Not only that, but the activists were arrested and will serve jail time for their outburst. Everything they did ended up costing them a lot and not advancing their cause. I believe the same thing happens when we react to an offense and do not respond appropriately. Before we react we never ask, "Will that reaction do any good?"

Listen, if your response to offense is changing the world, then hold on to it. If your offense is getting results and helping people love Jesus more, then I want to learn from you. If the way you are responding to offense isn't changing a heart, then I think it's time for you to learn another option. Jesus provides that option.

> "Love your enemies, do good to those who hate you, bless those who curse you, pray for those who mistreat you." Luke 6:27- 28.

The churches where I grew up had a war-like mindset against culture. The idea was that culture is wrong, and we need to fight against it. Christians should be separate from the world, but our weapons are not boycotts, and arguments on social media. Today, many

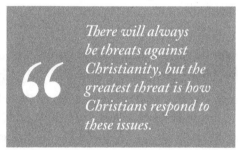

There will always be threats against Christianity, but the greatest threat is how Christians respond to these issues.

Christians feel threatened by a woke culture, socialism, and attacks on religious freedom. We have picked up the ball from the Christians in the 80s and continued our war on culture. There will always be threats against Christianity, but the greatest threat is how Christians respond to these issues. I agree with Bill Haslem, the former Governor of Tennessee when he said,

> "Christians are acting just like everyone else. We're just as likely to send a nasty message on the internet. We're just as likely to think we've

won a battle because we have the cleverest rhet-
oric on Twitter."

Everyone is offended, but no one is asking what good it is
doing! So, we have a culture war where people take sides, but
use the same strategies. There are serious offenses in the world,
but Christians shouldn't fight like everyone else. Our weapons
are love, doing good to our enemies, and praying for those
who mistreat us. As far as people who have changed the world
go, I think it would be difficult to find someone who did more
than Jesus. Jesus and the early Christians changed the world.
After Jesus rose from the grave, His followers were persecuted
severely. Despite the persecution, they ended up changing the
world because of how they responded to that persecution. They
didn't change the world with war or massive protests. They
weren't known for their boycotts, or outrage even though there
was a lot to cause outrage. The early Christians were known for
the way they loved people. Christians today need to learn how
to respond to the hurt of offense in the way Jesus taught. When
we model Jesus, we have something that no one else has, and
that is the ability to turn enemies into friends. You see, outrage
is quick to point out how wrong the other person or side of the
argument is. Love, on the other hand, can deal with offense in
a healthy way. Because offense is a hurt, we justify our actions.
We think the person on the other side of our offense is an enemy
and thus deserves judgment. So, we continually get on this
hamster wheel of offense where we boycott, avoid, break up
with, yell at, post snarky memes online, and fight against those
who offend us. If you are tired of the fighting, then Jesus' way
is worth considering. If you are tired of seeing arguments that
don't result in a changed opinion, then Jesus' way is a better

option. It may not be natural to love your enemies, but it's so powerful! When we are offended, we want to push away or hurt the one who offended us. Instead of trying to fight against those who offend you, engage them with love. Love is the only thing powerful enough to turn an offensive enemy into a friend.

A REAL LIFE EXAMPLE

In 1992, Larry Trapp hit the front page of newspapers across the country. He was the Grand Dragon of the Ku Klux Klan. He lived in Lincoln, Nebraska, and was offended that a Jewish rabbi had moved to his neighborhood. For years, Larry Trapp terrorized Jewish Rabbi Weisser who had moved into his community. He sent hate mail, threatening phone calls, and bomb threats.

In a 1992 interview with *Time Magazine*, Larry Trapp said he had wanted to scare Rabbi Weisser into moving out of Lincoln. "As the state leader, the Grand Dragon, I did more than my share of work because I wanted to build the state of Nebraska into a state as hateful as North Carolina and Florida,"

Out of nowhere, Trapp did a 360 and changed completely. He burned his Nazi flags, destroyed his hate literature, and renounced the KKK. How does that kind of trans- formation happen? The answer may surprise you. It did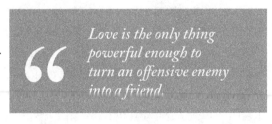

Love is the only thing powerful enough to turn an offensive enemy into a friend.

me. Larry Trapp started dying from diabetes. He was eventually confined to a wheelchair and couldn't take care of himself any longer and that's when Rabbi Weisser started showing him love. On a regular basis Rabbi Weisser would call Larry. Rabbi Weisser said, "I would say things like: 'Larry, there's a lot of love out there. You're not getting any of it. Don't you want some?' And hang up," He also left a message that said, "And, 'Larry, why do you love the Nazis so much? They'd have killed you first because you're disabled." Rabbi Weisser called once a week to give a message of love.

After consistently showing Larry Trapp love, the Rabbi was still shocked when his phone rang and on the other end was Larry Trapp. Larry said, "I want to get out of what I'm doing, and I don't know how."

That night, Rabbi Weisser and his wife went over to Larry Trapp's house. The three talked for hours and a close friendship formed. Soon, the Rabbi's home became a hospice for Mr. Trapp, who moved into one of their bedrooms as his health worsened. Rabbi Weisser and his wife became Larry Trapp's caretaker, confidant, and maybe even the most shocking...his friend. They showed him so much love that he couldn't help but love them back.

Are you kidding me? After years of real offense how would you respond to the person persecuting you? Many would respond with, "I'm glad he's dying! Serves him right! He is getting what he deserves." That is a natural response, but that would not have changed his life. In fact, I'm convinced Larry Trapp would have been buried with his offensive, racist, paraphernalia if it were not for the love of Rabbi Weisser. The only way this could happen is for the Rabbi to let go of his offense. Letting go of the offense doesn't mean that Larry Trapp was right. He was wrong and what he did was disgusting. But isn't this a better story than the alternative? Imagine this headline,

"Larry Trapp was a racist, so Rabbi Weisser boycotted him. Larry died."

No one would be inspired by that version of the story.

Like Larry Trapp, many people may want to get out of what they are doing, but they don't know how. I think many people see the division in the world and want to do something different, but they don't know how. I see people struggling relationally but do not know how to change. We cannot change other people, so we are going to have to work on ourselves. Who is the Larry Trapp in your life? Who offends you? Who do you consider to be an enemy? Jesus challenges us to love our enemies. I know there are offensive people out there. We cannot escape them, but we can ask what good our offense is doing. Imagine living in a world where you engage those who offend you with love? When we ask what good our offense is going to do, it helps us think through how to respond to those who offend us. If my response to an offense is going to push someone away, then I should rethink it. If my offense is going to lead me to act un-Christ-like, I should rethink it. Larry Trapp lived an offensive life. He was changed because Rabbi Weisser responded to offense with love.

I know it is easier to simply blame everyone else for all the issues, but that doesn't get great results. At times what we label offense is simply not getting our way. I see Christians getting offended and jumping from one church to the next, never dealing with the offense and leaving a trail of unresolved issues and broken relationships. You may have never had to deal with a KKK leader like Rabbi Weisser, but I'm guessing you've had to deal with a relative that votes differently than you. That person drives you crazy because of their outspoken beliefs. You may not even label it offense, but it is. I've seen people hold onto offense because they did not make the worship team at church. I've seen people hold onto an offense because the pastor did not meet their expectations. Maybe you've been offended because a leader made a decision you did not agree with. Maybe you've been offended because someone did not include you. Maybe you were offended because someone sins differently than you. I believe we are way more sensitive than we like to admit.

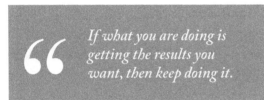

If what you are doing is getting the results you want, then keep doing it.

Offense is all around us. We may label it as being annoyed, toxic, or difficult, but even if you are not ranting online during political season there is something or someone that offends you. When that happens you will be tempted to react. I want to challenge you to react in a way that attempts to restore the relationship, and lead the other person to experience the love of Jesus.

At the end of the day, it comes down to results. If what you are doing is getting the results you want, then keep doing it. If you find you have thriving relationships that are filled with unity, then please keep doing what you are doing. If being offended is helping you win people, please keep doing it. If being offended is helping you love Jesus, love others, and make a difference then please write that book. Let me know when you do, and I'll buy it. If your offense is not winning people over, then will you be open to trying something else? It starts by asking, "What good is my offense doing?"

Questions:

1. When it comes to culture, what is your natural reaction? Is it more in line with going to war with culture, or is it more in line with embracing culture?

2. If you were Rabbi Weisser, how would you have responded to Larry Trapp?

3. Based on Jesus' words in Luke 6:27-28, what are the weapons we should use to fight against culture?

4. How should Jesus' sacrifice impact our desire to love our enemies?

5. Who do you know that could use the love of Jesus? What would it look like to start a relationship with that person?

CHAPTER 2

THE ULTIMATE PROBLEM
WITH OFFENSE

"Slacktivism – taking a stand that costs you
absolutely nothing." –Brant Hansen.

It is important to ask, "What good is my offense doing?"
According to researcher Arthur Brooks, our offense does
little good. In fact, being offended may actually prevent us from
doing good in the world. In his book Arthur C. Brooks looks
at America's charity divide to determine who gives and who
doesn't give to charity. His research is interesting.

> "It turns out that the people who are often the
> most indignant voices in protest of injustice are
> the least likely to part with their own resources
> to do anything about it." – Arthur C. Brooks
> from the book *Who Really Cares*?

The people who are often the most indignant voices in
protest of an injustice are the least likely to part with their
own resources. Why? My theory is because being offended is
exhausting. The mental energy that it takes from being offended

is a burden. When we get offended and reply in anger, it can blindly lead us to believe that we have done something productive. A temper tantrum may get someone to pay attention, but it won't change hearts. So, we get offended, and then dump that offense into the world, expecting it to change something. We rant, put up a quick Facebook post in anger, vent to someone who will listen, and then we feel better. There is a great chance that nothing has changed, but now that we feel better, we can move on to the next thing that offends us.

SLACKTAVISM

There are so many things that can offend us today; the way people vote, the personal choices people make, the fact that some people put the milk in the cereal bowl first and then put in the cereal. There are rules of order and right and wrong. Whenever I see someone put milk in the bowl before the cereal, I just want to know who hurt you so badly. I kid, I kid. There is a lot to get offended by in our world. However, the people I know who are truly making a difference are so busy changing the world they don't have time to comment on every offense.

In his book *Unoffendable*, Brant Hansen coins a term that I often use.

> "Slacktavism – taking a stand that costs you absolutely nothing." –Brant Hansen.

In our modern world of social media, it's easy to become a slacktivist. There is this social pressure to have an opinion about every global crisis. It feels like there is a race to show how much we care. Whenever an event happens, it seems as if there is this unspoken pressure to post support or to oppose the event by posting something on social media. I like what a psychotherapist says about this,

> "You are not morally obligated to comment on
> every global crisis." –Seerut K. Chawla

It's okay to not have an opinion. It's okay to have an opinion and not share it. It's okay to reserve comment and wait for more information to surface.

Brant Hansen's point about Slacktivism is that so often we take a stand, but it's nothing more than a publicity stunt. To really change the world, it is going to cost something.

Venting online may temporarily make us feel better, but it rarely convinces or changes anyone else. When someone rants, you'll see they gather a crowd of people who already agree with them. Until you are willing to put some money, time, or true effort towards changing things, don't fool yourself into thinking that your stance actually makes a difference in convincing those with whom you disagree. An opinion rarely changes things. We rant, yell, boycott, unfriend, and block, but rarely ask if such actions are helping to change the world. The mental energy exerted from being offended takes a toll on us.

"What if the Devil's plan is to keep us all so distracted with personal offenses that we feel too exhausted to actually make a difference? How would he do that? He would get us so focused on being offended that we exert lots of energy complaining, and in return we would be too tired to make a difference. Offense is everywhere. We get to choose if we want to open the door when it knocks."–Rob Shepherd.

Did I just quote myself? Yes, yes, I did. Quotes tend to stand out more than written text, and I really want you to get this. At some point, humans started to believe that unless they are angry or offended, they cannot change the world. There is so much offense, and if that is all it takes to change the world, then we would be living in paradise. Instead, there is lots of offense and very little effort to make the world better. It starts by asking, "What good is my offense doing?" The next step is to be devoted to something so compelling you don't have time to be offended.

THE OTHER WAY

"Our people must learn to devote themselves
to doing what is good, in order to provide for
urgent needs and not live unproductive lives."
(Titus 3:14).

Being offended can lead to an unproductive life. It can lead to slacktivism. Christians are called to devote themselves to doing what's good. I guess you could make a case that being offended about things is a good thing, but I'll need you to write that book. From my perspective, those who complain the most are the ones who are most easily offended, and those who are easily offended tend to spend more time complaining than creating good. Be so busy making a difference that you don't have time to complain about other people.

Here's a question for you. Are you devoted to doing what's good? The Scripture says that we must learn to devote ourselves to doing what is good. That means it's not natural. You were not created to simply exist. God has created you to bring Heaven to earth. God's plan is to use Christians to change the world.

I used to feel guilty when I would go to the grocery store and they would ask me if I would like to give an additional dollar to some very sad cause. I would often give, but it wasn't out of joy. It was because I felt like I was going to be judged by the 16-year-old who just bagged my Frosted Flakes. I no longer feel guilty, and here is the reason why. My wife and I have committed to doing good in the world. We can't do everything, but we can do something. We have a few strategic partners at our church whom we give to generously. We make sure to give above our regular tithe to make a difference. I know the money we give is going to organizations that we trust. I know our resources are truly helping people because we give to organizations with whom we have a relationship. We give consistently and intentionally. I don't have to feel bad when I choose not to give an extra dollar at the grocery store because I know I give in other ways.

It's similar with offense. There are lots of things to be offended by, and there is even pressure to be offended by the things that offend others. I know as a human I have limited space to care. I can't care about everything. I can't pour my life into every issue and cause. What I can do is intentionally commit to make a difference in a few causes. It means that I choose to pour my energy into a few selective things that will make a difference.

The causes that I care the most about involve children, the homeless, or the local church. That means that I can choose to not become passionate about other causes. It doesn't mean other causes aren't valid or important. They are important, but God didn't call me to every issue, and I don't have the energy to be passionate about everything. I can only give in a way that makes a difference to a few strategic things. Notice the verse says that we are to learn to be devoted to do good… "in order to provide for urgent needs."

In order to not be a slactivist, we must learn to be committed to doing good. We do this when we find what we are passionate about and intentionally give our time and money to that cause. What is a problem that you see in the world? What can you do to make the problem better? Maybe you can't start a new organization, or give lots of money, but you can do something. Since helping kids is one of my passions, I want to make sure that I'm giving some time and money towards issues involving kids.

Doing something productive is important because it helps us not be so critical. When we are less critical we become less offended. There are professional critics who get paid to share their opinion on someone else's work. I often say it like this, "There are directors and critics." When making a movie the director is a big deal. It takes a team of people to make a film, but ultimately the responsibility of how good a film is falls to the director. At the same time there are movie critics. Their job is to critique someone else's work. I don't know about you, but I don't want to be known for being a critic. There is a place for critics. They can help us make decisions on what movies to go to or what restaurants to dine in, but critics aren't known for what they create. Way too many people are critics and not directors. When you are a director you are creating something. The energy it takes to create something helps us remain productive. As Christians we should aim to be so productive we don't have time to be offended. Some people have made it their spiritual gift to criticize everything. Whenever I meet someone that is stuck in this mode I think, "They need to get busy changing the world." So let me ask you, what type of person do you want to be? Do you want to be a director who creates or a critic who tears down? This is how we follow Paul's command to devote ourselves to doing good.

FEED ONE

When I look at the people who are doing amazing work at changing the world for Jesus, I continue to see how they are some of the least offendable people I know. They are doing what Paul challenges us to do when he writes, "Our people must learn to devote themselves to doing what is good." If you remember from the verse above, Paul says the reason we must learn to be devoted to doing what is good is so that we don't live unproductive lives. Slacktivists live very unproductive lives. I'd argue that when we are committed to doing good in the world, we won't have as much time to be offended.

We all have limited capacity and when we lead with offense, I believe it exhausts us from doing the hard work of making a difference. In order not to be a slacktivist, we must commit to doing the hard work of sacrificing in order to see the world change. True change costs us something.

My ministry coach is one of my favorite people on the planet. His name is Chris Sonksen, and you'll find quotes from him sprinkled throughout my books and social media. Chris is one of the most positive people I know. It's no surprise that he is also one of the people who inspires me the most. He inspires me because he is out in the world actually making a difference. Chris helped start an initiative called FeedOne. His story is inspiring, and I want to share a portion of it.

We were supporting children in Haiti, and I had the opportunity to go on a trip to see what we were doing. I was taken to a school (which was basically brick walls, cement floor, and holes in the walls for ventilation. There were maybe 60-70 kids in the school room. They were having chapel. Most of the kids were probably 6-10 years old. I was on the stage with the principal, and in their language, he said, "The man standing up here is the pastor of the church who is helping to take care of you. He is one of the reasons you are receiving your meals each day. The kids spontaneously ran up to the stage, tackled me, started hugging me and kissing me and in their broken English were saying, "Thank you for our food".

When the kids went back to their seats, I noticed through the holes in the walls that there were kids observing us from the outside. I was told, "They are looking in and hoping there might be some leftover food". Side note: I was the one selected to go outside and tell the kids, "Try again tomorrow; there is no food left." I asked why they don't join the school. They said, "It takes $10 per month to get in the school, so they can learn, hear about Jesus, and get a meal.

On my way home, God spoke to me. He said, "You are giving money through your church, but you are not giving time or influence". I spoke to the director of Convoy of Hope and said, "I would like to do more". The result was the creation of an initiative out of Convoy called, "Feed One". It comes from what Mother Theresa said, "If you can't feed a hundred, then just "Feed one." — Chris Sonksen.

LET'S WRAP THIS UP

I'm continually inspired by Chris! I can't think of a single time he has ranted online. He doesn't spend his time arguing or debating people. Instead, he is busy changing the world.

Chris committed to change the world through the FeedOne initiative, and they are doing amazing work. You may never start an organization, an initiative, or even go on a mission trip, but I would highly encourage you to dedicate yourself to sacrificing something for the kingdom of God. The world is so negative, and so many people are offended by so many things, that it takes intentional effort to counter all the noise. The reason a majority of people I know are making such a difference in the world is because they are not easily offended. They are focused on something bigger than themselves. When you are actively changing the world, it is difficult to make time to get personally offended. For more information on FeedOne, visit FeedOne.com.

Questions:

1. What is something that truly offends you? What would it look like to make a difference in this area?

2. Think about your salvation story. In what ways has Jesus forgiven you? Is it possible to show others the same grace Jesus has given you?

3. What does it look like to put a relationship before an offense?

4. What was your biggest takeaway from this chapter?

CHAPTER 3

HUMBLE PIE TASTES BETTER THAN OFFENSIVE CAKE

"Now Moses was a very humble man, more humble than anyone else on the face of the earth." –Moses

In order to ask what good an offense does, we are going to need a serious dose of humility. Because offense is a hurt, we will naturally focus on the person on the other side of the offense. I continue to hear people complain about how offended everyone is these days. I'd say it's a natural by-product of being self-indulgent. A result of removing God from our culture is that we all become even more self-centered. God gives us someone other than ourselves to focus on. Without God, we naturally think about ourselves, our perspectives, and our worldviews, and elevate those views over others. On the other hand it is difficult to be offended when you practice humility.

While writing this book, I went to Facebook to ask what things offend people. Here is what was shared in the comments:

Traffic, the band Nickelback, President _____ (insert name of one who didn't get your vote), the word moist, abortion, gun rights, Liberals, Conservatives, strongly opinionated people, Christians misrepresenting Jesus, rudeness, tardiness, when someone doesn't text you back, when someone calls you instead of texting you, Twitter, bullying, slow drivers in the left lane, littering, loud chewing, when someone uses the word retarded as a slur towards someone else, racism, sexism, xenophobia, unfair treatment of others, poor service at a restaurant, weak WIFI signal, and finally... people saying, "That triggers me." Seriously, some people are triggered by the word "trigger." Facebook did not disappoint.

There are so many things that offend us, and that is one thing that makes offense difficult to nail down. What offends one person doesn't bother another person. It would be easier to battle against offense if it was universal. It's not. It's not universal because offense is tied to a personal hurt. As humans, we tend to only get offended at the things that impact us. We are selfish creatures by nature. I know this is true for myself. For most of my life I was easily offended. When someone didn't respond the way I wanted them to, when someone said something that I didn't like, when I didn't get my way, or when I felt left out, I would get offended. One of the massive benefits to following Jesus is that it leads us to take our eyes off of ourselves. I didn't set out to become less offended, but I became less offended the more I matured in my faith with Jesus. Without humility, we will make a bigger deal of things that offend us, be less willing to listen to other perspectives, and more willing to condemn those who disagree with us. Humility is the antidote to offense.

Without humility, our offense is not that noble. So often when we get offended, it is because we didn't get our way. We are offended when we don't get invited. We are offended when people don't give us the credit we think we deserve. We become offended when someone has a different opinion than us. Think about this for just a second. Why does someone with a different political view irritate you so much? Or how about this, why does a different opinion from your parents irritate you so much? We are offended when we think something is not fair. Have you ever noticed how the only time people complain that something is not fair is when they aren't getting something good that others are? Just once, I'd like to hear my kids say, "Dad, thank you for this special treat that only I am getting. Sorry, I cannot take it because it would not be fair to my sibling whom I love." I don't know a single child in the world who would express such a

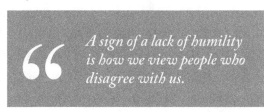

A sign of a lack of humility is how we view people who disagree with us.

statement. It's because we were born selfish. No one had to teach a child to say, "Mine" or "That's not fair."

Speaking of siblings, Jesus' brother, James, gives us some insight on this when he writes:

> What causes fights and quarrels among you? Don't they come from your desires that battle within you? You desire but do not have, so you kill. You covet but you cannot get what you want, so you quarrel and fight. You do not have because you do not ask God (James 4:1-2).

When we get offended, our brains lock in on how the other person hurt us. We become blind to our own selfish desires and to the part we play in the matter. We think that the issue is the other person, but James shares that the real issue is within. We fight because we are selfish. We quarrel because we are prideful. Did you notice what James said at the end of the verse? We don't have because we don't ask God, and we don't ask God because our pride tells us we are self-sufficient. We don't go to God first because we think we can handle it on our own. We don't have humility because we are constantly fighting to be self-sufficient.

A sign of a lack of humility is how we view people who disagree with us. If everyone who disagrees with you is an idiot, then you have a pride problem. We are way more prideful than we'd like to admit. I believe that a lot of our offense is due to our pride. We don't like to ask for help, but then become offended when others don't know that we need help. We don't like to be corrected even though we know we aren't perfect. The following quote is just as challenging as it is helpful.

> "Few want to hear this, but it's true, and it can be enormously helpful in life: If you're constantly being hurt, offended, or angered, you should honestly evaluate your inflamed ego."

— Brant Hansen, *Unoffendable: How Just One Change Can Make All of Life Better*

Ouch! This is why humility is the antidote to offense. When we are offended, we focus on the other person, but we need to do some self-evaluation. The key to becoming less offended is not making everyone else just like you. Even if everyone was just like you, you'd find a way to be offended by them. I'm convinced we'd find a way to be offended because so much of our offense is tied to our ego. The key to becoming less offended is humility. We are wired to think about ourselves, and because of that, we are more likely to get offended when someone does

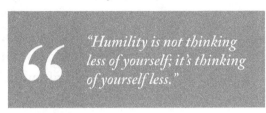

"Humility is not thinking less of yourself; it's thinking of yourself less."

something we do not like. When we become offended, we focus on the other person, but our focus is in the wrong place. When we only focus on others, our offense becomes a moving target. The answer to offense is not to destroy everyone who disagrees. That is unsustainable and will result in a very lonely world. What if instead of being offended, we could simply not get offended? Wait! Is that an option? It's probably not an option to become completely impervious to offense, but when we gain humility, we will become offended a lot less.

If the idea of humility sounds like a magical fairy tale, please know it's very real. I've tested it out. The key for me was learning what it meant to be humble. Once I understood that humility was not some weak sauce insecurity, I was able to embrace humility.

WHAT IS HUMILITY?

We live in a society that has perfected the selfie. We are wired to think about ourselves and our culture has rewarded that. I recently watched a TikTok where a man tried to take a selfie with wild rams. As if a picture of these amazing animals wasn't enough, this man got out of his car and tried to get the rams to pose with him. This was all filmed by someone else who ended up going viral on TikTok for the video. Thankfully, some other onlooker can be heard yelling in the background to the man attempting to pose with wild rams. It takes a few seconds, and one big fake out attack from one of the rams, for the selfie guy to realize this is a horrible idea. How do we become more humble when all of our culture is catering to our desire to take selfies with wild rams?

So many words get highjacked today, so it's important to define the word "humility". I love the definition of humility given by Pastor Rick Warren,

"Humility is not thinking less of yourself; it's thinking of yourself less."

Now imagine having that definition of humility as you respond to offense. This is the problem with humility; it requires us to think about ourselves less. Notice the definition is not to think less of yourself. You can be confident and humble. Humility is not putting yourself down, becoming a doormat, or a spiritual form of insecurity. Humility is thinking of others more than you think about yourself. When we get offended, all we can do is think about how it hurt us. Humility helps us see that on the other side of our hurt is a person Jesus loves. True humility is loving someone no matter their differences. If you only love those who you agree with then you are creating an echo chamber of people that are just like you. That only works if you are always right. It may be difficult to admit but no one is always right, even those who act like it. The only way to love those we disagree with is to have a serious dose of humility.

We are wired to think about ourselves. Humility is the only force powerful enough to keep us from becoming manically self-absorbed. This is why following Jesus is so important to humility. When you follow Jesus, your focus isn't on yourself; it's on Jesus. When we have humility, we have an accurate view of ourselves from Jesus' perspective.

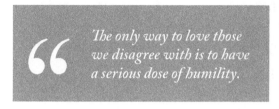

The only way to love those we disagree with is to have a serious dose of humility.

We are far more loved than we can ever imagine, and far more jacked up than we care to admit. Following Jesus allows us to see ourselves as He does, and it allows us to see others as He sees them as well.

PETER GETS IT

Peter was one of Jesus' closest friends and is a perfect example of how following Jesus can change a person. Peter often reacted first and asked questions second. He is the guy, after all, who tried to fight a mob of Roman soldier's by himself. I'm not sure what Peter was aiming at, but he managed to chop off a soldier's ear. He either has amazing aim and his target was the ear, or he was just wielding that sword willy nilly and just so happened to only hit the soldiers ear. Either way Peter reacted first and asked questions second. It's only after Jesus heals the amputated ear that Peter realizes he was in the wrong. After Jesus rises from the dead, Peter is changed. He's humbled. He is not as quick to draw a sword or to put his foot in his mouth. The following words come from a guy who has embraced humility even though it didn't come naturally to him.

> "All of you, clothe yourselves with humility toward one another, because, 'God opposes the proud but shows favor to the humble.' Humble yourselves, therefore, under God's mighty hand, that he may lift you up in due time" (1 Peter 5:5-6).

Peter's challenge is to clothe yourself with humility towards each other. To clothe oneself takes intentional effort. No one wakes up fully clothed and thinks, "Why am I not naked?" To get dressed is an intentional decision and so is becoming more humble. When we intentionally carve out time to serve others, put others first, pray, and read the Bible, we are making intentional choices to clothe ourselves with humility. We struggle so much in relationships because we naturally put our wants, desires, and opinions ahead of other people. The fear is, if we don't fight for what we want, then we won't get what we want. That's a real fear. It is

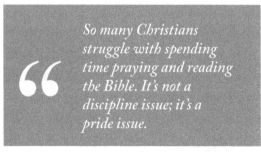

So many Christians struggle with spending time praying and reading the Bible. It's not a discipline issue; it's a pride issue.

somewhat ironic that the reason we don't want to be humble is because we fear we won't get what we want. I've found that when we put others first, they are way more agreeable.

When we put others first, we end up compromising, but the end result is better.

Peter gives us some insight into God. God opposes the proud but shows favor to the humble. That's interesting. To humble ourselves under God's mighty right hand means that we live as if God is in control. We humble ourselves when we pray because we are showing that we are not in control. We humble ourselves when we read the Bible because we show that we don't have all the answers. So many Christians struggle with spending time praying and reading the Bible. It's not a discipline issue; it's a pride issue. Humans are wired to be self-reliant, and this is why so many people wait until they hit rock bottom to cry out to God. When we hit rock bottom, we are finally humble enough to admit we need some help. Yet, what do we do in the meantime? If you are a Christian, and you agree with my assessment that our offense problem is really a lack of humility problem, then what do we do? How does following Jesus make us more humble? That's a great question. Thanks for asking it.

JESUS, THE GREAT AMERICAN HERO

The key to becoming more humble is to follow Jesus. I want to explore what that means. You see, there is a difference between following Jesus and believing in Jesus. You can believe that Jesus existed, but in order to experience Jesus — you have to follow Him. That means that we lay down our rights. If Jesus agrees with everything you do, you probably are not following Jesus. In some circles, following Jesus has become a universal chameleon that adapts to all of our desires. In this version of Jesus, He looks like us, accepts what we like, doesn't support those who disagree with us, and passionately supports our causes. I saw the following online, and I don't think it was meant to be funny. I never know what to trust on the Internet, but this image helps make my point.

Jesus is not an American...sweaty. I think she meant sweetie. Jesus is not a Republican. Jesus is not a Democrat. Jesus is not waiting around to see what offends you, then changing His opinions to match yours. Everyone likes Jesus when they can make him fit their agenda. The problem is Jesus is not like bacon. Bacon goes with everything...unless you are a vegetarian. Bacon doesn't really go with vegetarians. For those who are meatetarians[3] you can have bacon with breakfast, bacon for lunch, bacon for dinner, and even chocolate covered bacon for dessert. Bacon is so versatile that it goes with eggs just as well as it does a cheeseburger. As great as bacon is, Jesus is not like bacon. He doesn't adapt who He is to fit our offense. You are not the center of the universe; Jesus is. Jesus is the main

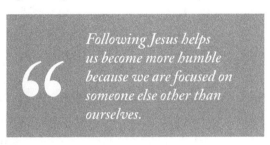

Following Jesus helps us become more humble because we are focused on someone else other than ourselves.

course, and you are the bacon adapting to fit with Him. Okay, that illustration has made me hungry, but I hope you get the point. When we study Scripture and get to know Jesus, we see that He is asking us to lay down our identity, rights, opinions, and offenses to follow Him. Because Jesus is the main character, following Him results in thinking about ourselves a lot less. When that happens, we gain humility.

---

[3] This is not a typo. I believe I made this word up.

LET'S MAKE THIS PRACTICAL

The idea of this chapter is that we get offended more easily when we lack humility. Following Jesus helps us become more humble because we are focused on someone else other than ourselves. Here are three practical ideas to help you follow Jesus more. I believe the natural result will be more humility and less offense.

Three Practical Ideas to follow Jesus:

1. Prioritize God by reading the Bible and praying every day. Remember what Peter said, "Humble yourselves, therefore, under God's mighty hand, that he may lift you up in due time." Starting your day with God, before you get out of bed, is intentionally making an effort to think about yourself less. My rule of thumb is I don't get out of bed until I've read the Bible. I started a rule like this in college. In college I wouldn't eat until I had read the Bible. My motto was feed the soul first. This helped me until cell phones were invented. I found myself waking up and checking social media first. Then I would have to rush out of bed in order to not be late to work. So I created a new rule for myself. Read the Bible first. When I first wake up the first app I open is YouVersion. It's a Bible app and has thousands of Bible studies. I pray and read the Bible first thing when I wake up. Social media can wait.

2. Serve at your local church. Serving isn't always easy because it forces you to think about others. At the same time serving is rewarding because it forces you to think

about others. You may not enjoy serving regularly, but remember it's not all about you. Serving is a small way to give back to God and get your mind off yourself. Plus, a benefit of serving at church is that you get to connect with other believers. Serving at your church is a great way to do what we discussed in the last chapter — being committed to doing what is good.

3. Form relationships with people who you disagree with. Jesus did just this. Jesus didn't hang out with people who already agreed with Him. He wasn't only friends with people who voted like, looked like, and thought like Him. It's like inspirational speaker and author Bob Goff says, "The way we love difficult people is some of the best evidence that the tomb was really empty." If you cannot have a relationship with someone who you disagree with, you have a humility problem. All relationships are difficult, but almost nothing stretches us more than learning to love difficult people.

HUMILITY PRAYER

The following is a sample prayer for humility. I encourage you to copy it and place it where you can pray it every day. Take a picture of it and save it on your phone, write it out and put it on your nightstand, print it and put it on the bathroom mirror. The point is to put it some place you'll see it and pray it daily.

God, I am far too often influenced by what others think of me. I am always pretending to

be either richer or smarter or nicer than I really
am. Please prevent me from trying to attract
attention. Don't let me gloat over praise on one
hand or be discouraged by criticism on the other.
Nor let me waste time weaving imaginary situa-
tions in which the most heroic, charming, witty
person present is myself. Show me how to be
humble of heart, like you. —Author Unknown

Questions:

1. Before reading this chapter, how would you
   define humility?

2. What do you do when what Jesus says goes against
   what you feel is fair?

3. Does what typically offends you also offend Jesus?
   Why or why not?

4. Is it possible for you to show care for someone with
   whom you disagree? What would that look like?

CHAPTER 4

WHEN OFFENSE LEADS TO CRUCIFIXION

"The feeling of being offended is a warning indicator that is showing you where to look within yourself for unresolved issues." –Bryant H. McGill.

To ask what good is accomplished by our offense takes humility. We don't naturally ask that question because in our hurt, we don't care what our response does. When we are hurt, we focus on the one who hurt us, and lose sight of our part in the story.

When you respond in your hurt, you can do a lot of damage. Offense can seem like a small thing, but because the root of offense is hurt, even the smallest offenses can become major wounds. When you don't deal with an offense, the hurt can grow. What started out as a minor offense can easily lead to the filter in which you view the other person. I've seen grown adults who go to church and love Jesus, respond very un-Christ like to offense. I've seen Christians leave churches, break off relationships, and act a fool all because of an offense that is not healed. It may start off as a small offense. It could be not getting the recognition you think you deserve. It may have started from being corrected, or maybe the offense started because you were left out. Maybe the offense started because of the way someone spoke to you, or maybe it was because of something they said. Intentional or not, when someone offends us there is a wound. When the wound doesn't heal, we start to view the other person through our hurt. Instead of seeing all the good they do, we can only focus on the hurt they caused.

Because offense is a wound, if we are not careful, we will start to respond out of our hurt instead of out of the healing Jesus has done in us. When this happens, we will lash out in ways that do not represent Jesus. Because an offense starts as a wound, our sinful nature wants vengeance on whoever hurt us. Often, in our hurt, the justice that we want doesn't even match the crime. Even if the other person is truly offensive, we must guard our hearts from allowing hurt to remain unhealed. If we do not deal with the hurt that we have experienced, we will end up hurting others. I often think about the following quote:

> "If you never heal from what hurt you, you'll
> bleed on people who didn't cut you."–Unknown

I know that people have hurt you. It stinks! It may have been your parents, a spouse, people at church, or even a pastor who hurt you. Forgiving them and healing has little to do with them. Healing doesn't mean that you are justifying their actions. It means you aren't going to give them so much power over

> *"If you never heal from what hurt you, you'll bleed on people who didn't cut you." - Unknown*

you. Unforgiveness puts the person who hurt you in the place of offending you, constantly. When you forgive, you are taking away the offender's power to continually hurt you. This is a serious matter for Christians. Christians are called to forgive as we have been forgiven. We desperately want God's forgiveness while we clutch onto bitterness and hurt from those who have wounded us. If you have been forgiven from your sin by Jesus, then you are to return that gift by forgiving those who hurt you. Author Jackie Hill Perry says it like this, "Nobody can offend you more than you've offended God." Her point is that your sin is offensive to God, and yet He forgives. To receive that forgiveness from God, but then withhold it from others is the ultimate form of selfishness.

There are some serious offenses that have happened in the church, but there are also a lot of hurts that have a lot more to do with the offended person than the offense.

As mentioned in the last chapter, humility plays a big part in becoming less offended. Without humility, we will be offended more often. I've heard Christians describe the trauma they've experienced. I showed as much empathy as I could because I don't want to dismiss someone else's pain. When they finished talking, the trauma they referred to was more about them not getting their way. They talked as if they had been abused, but the reality of the situation was they didn't get their way. Without humility, offenses are more personal, and we respond to small offenses with big emotions. Without humility, we will allow wounds, no matter how small, to fester for years. When we don't find healing, we end up hurting others. If we are not careful, we will want others to hurt more than they hurt us. It's what I call, from offense to crucifixion.

41

FROM OFFENSE TO CRUCIFIXION

If you've read through the New Testament, you might be familiar with the time a woman anointed Jesus by pouring expensive perfume on Him. It's mentioned in Matthew and John. I've read it dozens of times, but it wasn't until recently that I saw how offense played a part in the story. It starts with how Jesus responds to the woman who poured perfume on Him. Watch carefully how an offense leads to a crucifixion. The following picks up right after the disciples see the women pour perfume on Jesus.

> When the disciples saw this, they were indignant. "Why this waste?" they asked. "This perfume could have been sold at a high price and the money given to the poor" (Matthew 26:8-9).

Did you catch how they responded? The disciples were indignant! From their perspective, this was a waste of money and could have been used to help the poor. That's something Jesus fully supports. So much of Jesus' ministry was and is to the poor. At first, it sounds as if this was a noble response to the woman's act of worship. To the disciples' surprise, Jesus doesn't share their opinion, and He rebukes them. Put yourself in their sandals for just a second. How would you feel if you thought you were doing something righteous for God and He rebuked you? I wonder how Jesus would respond to the things that offend us? I wonder if part of our problem is that we are loading with offense and asking Jesus to jump on board, instead of seeking to find out what truly offends God? Read how Jesus replies.

Aware of this, Jesus said to them, "Why are you bothering this woman? She has done a beautiful thing to me. The poor you will always have with you, but you will not always have me. When she poured this perfume on my body, she did it to prepare me for burial. Truly I tell you, wherever this gospel is preached throughout the world, what she has done will also be told, in memory of her (Matthew 26:10-13).

Jesus senses they are complaining and essentially says, "Matthew and John, get out your pens and write this down. What this woman is doing will be a part of my story."

Now, that's a story with which I am very familiar. However, it wasn't until recently when I was reading through the New Testament that I stumbled upon a new insight. The Gospel of John gives some more information about this account. Where Mathew is a little more general, John is specific.

But one of his disciples, Judas Iscariot, who was later to betray him, objected, "Why wasn't this perfume sold and the money given to the poor? It was worth a year's wages." He did not say this because he cared about the poor but because he was a thief; as keeper of the money bag, he used to help himself to what was put into it (John 12.4-6).

John isn't playing around. He calls out Judas! Not only does he call out Judas individually, he also takes this time to note that

Judas took care of the money and often stole from them. That helps us know why Jesus responded the way He did.

After Jesus rebuked the disciple, that we now know is Judas, the text says:

> Then one of the Twelve—the one called Judas Iscariot—went to the chief priests and asked, "What are you willing to give me if I deliver him over to you?" So, they counted out for him thirty pieces of silver. From then on Judas watched for an opportunity to hand him over (Matthew 26:14-16).

The "Then" makes me think Judas' response is in direct correlation to Jesus' correction. After this, Judas agrees to betray Jesus. In all my years of studying and preaching the Scriptures, I had never seen this. Judas was offended! He becomes offended

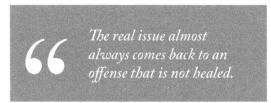

The real issue almost always comes back to an offense that is not healed.

because Jesus corrects him. Once Judas is corrected, he immediately seeks a way to get back at Jesus. In a few short moments, an offense leads to a crucifixion. Without humility, we are more likely to be offended. Like Judas, our offense can start from a minor disagreement. The hurt leads to a desire for justice. It's easy to judge Judas, but I'm not sure we are that different.

I've been a pastor long enough to see how offense leads to crucifixion. Often when someone shares with me concerns about their past church, they will bring up a list of things they disagreed with. I listen. I wait. At some point, they will reveal what the real issue is. The real issue almost always comes back to an offense that is not healed.

I've seen so much offense happen in the church world. The following are real life examples of reasons Christians have left a church. These examples are compiled from various churches across America.

- A woman on the worship was asked to wear leggings because her dress was too short. She became offended by this and left the church.

- A member of the usher team left because the church started blocking off seating in the back of the sanctuary. Their goal was to help people sit up closer. He was offended and attempted to lead a mini revolt.

- A man became offended because the pastor continued to add an "s" to the name of the program he led. He was very clear it was pronounced "Awana" not "Awanas."

- Small group leaders were asked to stop pushing their Multi-Level Marketing on their group. They were offended and left the church because of it.

- A woman in the choir had a cosmetic surgery to enhance her chest. Another woman became offended by the attention this woman was now getting. The drama that ensued over this ended up splitting the church.

- A woman was offended when the pastor was not available to do her mom's funeral. The pastor was on vacation, and the mom did not even go to his church. She left the church over this.

- A church held a surprise party for one of it's members at the church. After pictures were shown online a couple fussed at the pastor because they were not invited to the surprise party. When the pastor asked if they knew the person the party was for they said, "no." They left the church soon after.

- A family left a church because they found out other women at the church enjoyed watching the television show Downton Abbey.

- A family left the church because the pastor did not like the decorations they used for a stage design.

- A man was offended because the worship leader wore a t-shirt that featured the logo for the band The Rolling Stones.

- A woman applied for a job at a church and was offended that they did not hire her. She left soon after without saying a word to anyone.

- A couple walked out during a sermon because the pastor showed a movie clip from an R rated film. The film and the clip were not offensive. The fact that the movie was rated R is what made them leave.

- A family left because the pastor mentioned emotional health in his sermon. They felt that emotional health was not a spiritual issue and left the church over this.

Often the offense starts as a small wound. When it's not forgiven, the wound festers. From that moment on, the person views every situation through the hurt of that offense. Sometimes, it takes months, or even years, but eventually there is a long laundry list of issues that involve the church, and the person feels they have to leave. Along the way, they have forgotten what started it all, an offense.

But what if we didn't have to be offended? What if we did not have to react to every opinion? What if, we didn't have to get angry when others disagree with us? What if even in the face of real offense, we could remain cool and not react to our hurt? This is what following Jesus does for us. It takes the focus off of our own pain and helps us respond like Jesus.

Think about someone with whom you are frustrated, bitter, or have a broken relationship. How did it start? Did it start with someone not meeting your expectations? Did it start with you not getting your way? Was the person who hurt you truly evil? Specifically, did they wake up on that day (like a villain from a superhero movie) and set out to hurt you? Were you hurt because they didn't meet a need, expectation, or you didn't get your way? I've been hurt by people who had evil intentions, but I've also been hurt by people who did not intend harm. They weren't out to get me. I was hurt because I didn't get my way, have an expectation met, or because they weren't who I thought they were. When someone hurts you, it is natural to want to hurt them back. One of the ways we try to do that is to hold onto unforgiveness. The problem is, the only person you hurt is yourself.

When we refuse to forgive, we give the other person the power to continually hurt us. Because offense is a wound, it

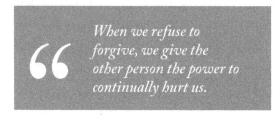

> *When we refuse to forgive, we give the other person the power to continually hurt us.*

can grow. When an offense isn't healed, it corrupts the soul like a cancer. For a moment, Judas felt justified in what he did to Jesus. After he saw the destruction he caused, he felt shame. When offended, we can write checks we regret cashing. I know hardly no one uses checks anymore, but you get the idea. We justify our actions because we feel hurt, but Jesus calls us to lay down our weapons of offense and forgive. Jesus says,

> "For if you forgive other people when they sin against you, your heavenly Father will also forgive you" (Matthew 6:14).

The hurt that you have experienced, whether it was small or big, needs to be forgiven. For Christians, our refusal to forgive has a direct correlation to our own forgiveness. When we lack humility, our pride convinces us that when others sin against us it is somehow different than when we sin against others. We want forgiveness when we sin and justice when others sin against us. Jesus offers us forgiveness and grace despite the ugliness of our sin. How dare we take the gift of forgiveness that Jesus has given us and refuse to pass it on to others!

The time is now! If you have someone in your life that you haven't forgiven, take a moment right now and forgive them as Jesus forgave you. It could go something like this:

"God, I don't have the strength to forgive _____.
You know what they did. It hurt, but I don't want
to continue to hurt. I forgive them for _____
like you have forgiven me. In Jesus name amen."

A MODERN EXAMPLE

In 1996, Keshia Thomas found herself in a very scary situation. Keshia was a senior in high school when she attended a peaceful protest in Ann Arbor, Michigan. A loud commotion grabbed her attention; she saw a man get pushed to the ground. The once peaceful crowd turned violent. As she watched the crowd kick and attack the man on the ground she said, "When they dropped him to the ground, it felt like two angels had lifted my body up and laid me down." A photographer captured the images of Keshia laying her body on top of the man to protect him from the crowd. It was an amazing, selfless act of courage. That is amazing, but those details are only part of the story. You see, Keshia was peacefully protesting a public march by the KKK. The peaceful protestors were separated from the parade of Klansmen fully dressed in their white hoods, Nazi paraphernalia, and confederate flags. At one point, a woman with a megaphone yells, "There's a Klansman in the crowd." Instantly, the peaceful crowd turns hostile. Shouts of "Kill the Nazi" come from the crowd. The man whom the crowd knocked down was wearing a Confederate flag shirt and had

Nazi tattoos. As a young black woman, Keshia could have justified joining in the attack. Why in the world would Keshia put her life on the line for the very people she was protesting? In her own words she said, "I knew what it was like to be hurt. The many times that has happened, I wished someone would have stood up for me." I can relate to those words.

The natural way to respond to an offense is to attack. When you follow Jesus, you have the humility to look past the hurt and see the person who hurt you. A person who is hurting himself is a person who is broken and in need of Jesus. Following Jesus causes us to focus on something other than ourselves. People will offend you. People will believe things that are stupid and wrong. People will have opinions that go against the teachings of Scripture. People are dumb. I know; I am one.

On the other side of the offense is a person who is hurting, and in need of Jesus' love. In your hurt, you may want them to feel pain. This is how offense turns to crucifixion. Our hurt wants others to pay the price, but that's not the way of Jesus. When we were hurting, Jesus reached down to help us. What if we changed our perspective on offense? What if instead of labeling the person who offended us as evil, we viewed them through the lens of compassion. The person who offended you is hurting, and because of Jesus, you can cover them with love. That, my friends, is how we change the world!

Questions:

1. Spend a few moments thanking Jesus out loud for the forgiveness He has shown you.

2. Is it easy or difficult for you to receive Jesus' forgiveness?

3. Is it easy or difficult for you to give forgiveness to others?

4. Is there someone you have struggled to forgive? How can Jesus' forgiveness help you forgive them?

5. What is your biggest takeaway from this chapter?

CHAPTER 5

JESUS WILL OFFEND WHAT OFFENDS YOU

"Guard against idols—yes, guard against all idols, of which surely the greatest is oneself." – Alexandra David-Neel

As Christians we have to be on guard about seeing the world through any lens other than the Gospel. The Gospel says that we are more sinful than we care to admit, but more loved than we could ever imagine! In America it is easy to try and combine multiple worldviews with Christianity. Many Americans have a mutt of a worldview. It's a combination of various morals, standards, and ideas. Truly following Jesus will lead you to choose who you will

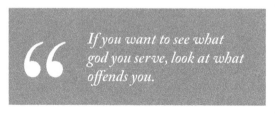

> *If you want to see what god you serve, look at what offends you.*

serve. Jesus will offend your American worldview. He will offend your political world view. He will offend your social world view and your ethnic world view. Many of these world-views become a part of our identity and when that happens they become an idol. If you want to see what god you serve, look at what offends you.

Judas' god was money. When Jesus rebuked him, he was offended. Your god may be physical appearance, perfectionism, material possessions, politics, race, or gender, to name a few. If there is anything in your life that is untouchable, it's a god.

Don't miss the point of this. If you want to see what god you serve, look at what offends you. Is your god money? Is your god being right? Is your god politics? Is your god your opinion? Is your god your church denomination? Is your god your race?

AT SOME POINT JESUS WILL OFFEND YOU

At some point, Jesus will offend you.

To the rich, He says, "Give."

To the sinner, He says, "Repent."

To the self-righteous, He says, "I don't know you."

To those who have been wronged, He says, "Forgive as I have forgiven you."

To the judgmental, He says, "Drop your stones."

To those in power, He says, "Become a servant."

To those who hate, He says, "Love."

To those who are oppressed, He says, "Go the second mile."

To those who think they are in, He says, "You are out."

To those who we think should be out, He says, "You are in."

Without humility, we walk away from Jesus. After all, you can only serve one master. If Jesus is master, then it makes sense that He makes the rules. When you are the center of your own story, anyone who disagrees with you is in danger of becoming an enemy. Humans are idol-making machines. We can make an idol out of anything, and it normally starts with something we love...ourself. I think the following quote from Pastor C.J. Mahaney is convicting and has a lot of truth to it.

> "Sometimes, you might perceive an offense even when no one has sinned against you — in which case the only thing that was 'offended' was your own pride, self-centeredness, or some other idol in your heart."

Jesus will challenge your idols. He desires your whole heart! To get to our hearts Jesus will offend your idols. If you are not careful, you will resist Jesus' correction.

CORRECTION AND HUMILITY

"If someone corrects you, and you feel offended, then you have an ego problem." –Matthew McConaughey.

Alright, alright, alright. Did I just quote actor, Academy Award winner, and Lincoln Motor Company spokesman Matthew McConaughey? Yes, I did. No one enjoys being corrected, but if you cannot be corrected without feeling offended, then you have an idol. We cannot grow without correction. If Jesus approves of everything we do, then we aren't following Jesus. Jesus will offend us when we refuse to remove our idols.

Make no mistake about it, you can believe in Jesus and still make everything about yourself. You can believe in Jesus and still live for yourself. Have you ever met a Christian who was a jerk? I know I have. I have multiple examples of people who claim to follow Jesus, but are jerks online. There is a massive difference between following Jesus and believing in Jesus. Just being in close proximity to Jesus isn't enough to change your life. There were lots of people who were in close proximity to Jesus, yet their lives were not changed. I believe a way to tell if you are following after Jesus vs. simply believing in Him is to see how you react to offense. When you follow after Jesus, you will work to respond to offense in a way that honors Him. When you simply believe in Him, it won't change how you react to being offended. In fact, because offense is a hurt, you will look to hurt the person who offended you. It may be a little hurt like giving them the silent treatment or being passive aggressive, or it may be a big hurt that comes in the form of name calling, ending the relationship, or even physical violence.

BACK TO JUDAS

To think, this all started with Judas saying he wanted to do something noble like save money for the poor. Like Judas, we can fool ourselves into thinking we are noble. When we get offended, it's natural to want to focus on the offense. It's natural to lash out at the person who hurt us. When this happens,

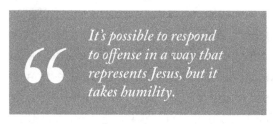

It's possible to respond to offense in a way that represents Jesus, but it takes humility.

we end up writing emotional checks we regret cashing. Judas did. His hurt led him to betray Jesus, but once he calmed down, he realized what he had done. At that point, it was too late.

Judas is an example of what can happen when humans experience offense. He was a Jesus follower. He was one of twelve men Jesus handpicked. He stepped away from it all after he got offended. If Judas is the human example of offense, then Jesus is our Godly example. On Jesus' last night, He washed his twelve disciples' feet. Included in that twelve was Judas. The very man who (in just a few minutes) would betray Him, Jesus took the time to serve. Jesus knew Judas was going to betray Him, yet He still served him. It may not be easy, but Jesus shows us that it's possible. It's possible to serve those with whom you disagree. It's possible to love those who wrong you. It's possible to respond to offense in a way that represents Jesus, but it takes humility.

LET'S GET PRACTICAL

The next time you get offended, do this. Take a deep breath and then ask yourself, "Why does this bother me so much?" Start there. Don't start by composing an email to the person who upset you. Don't start by replying on social media. Please don't start by finding an article that supports your view and then passive aggressively share it on social media. Don't attack others. Just sit and listen to your thoughts.

Behind every offense is an idol. Behind every idol is a selfish motive. Behind every selfish motive is a hurt.

So often we argue with others and at the end of the confrontation no opinions are changed. Because offense is a hurt we react without asking if it did any good. You can do better, and it starts with figuring out why this offense bothers you so much.

If you are on the other side of someone's offense, you can do the same thing. Start by listening. If you feel

> *Behind every offense is an idol. Behind every idol is a selfish motive. Behind every selfish motive is a hurt.*

attacked, ask why this bothers you so much? After you listen, show that you have heard the other person. Empathy goes a long way! You can say something like, "I can see this greatly upsets you. Help me understand why this offends you." Now, some people won't understand the question, and they may bom bard you with talking points, and more arguing. Stand your ground. Show empathy, and then ask again.

Some people are just angry. Some people are unhealthy. Some people just want to fight. You have to decide who to ignore and who to engage. My point is that when you engage, start with getting to the heart of the offense. You'll learn a lot, and it will help you have empathy.

You see, Jesus loves the victim and the perpetrator. Jesus loves the racist. Jesus loves the hateful. Jesus loves the Internet troll. Jesus doesn't just love people who agree with Him. He loves the whole world. If your world isn't big enough for people who disagree with you, then you have become your own idol. If you want to see what god you serve, look at what offends you. Jesus loves you even though you are imperfect. Jesus loves you even though you have blatantly chosen to sin instead of follow Him. Jesus loves you, all of you. He loves your entire being, not just the nice parts that other people love. Jesus loves you so much that He is willing to refine you. If you want to follow Jesus, you have to understand that there is no room for another god. That includes you. Jesus loves you, so you can represent Him to others. This is why He modeled loving enemies. Our goal, as Christians, should be to love people in a way that wins some to Jesus, and still love people who don't receive Jesus.

At some point, Jesus will offend you because He will ask you to forgive the person who hurt you. He will ask you to serve the person who offended you. He will ask you to love your enemies. He will ask you to repent of your sin. Be careful. If Jesus is anything less than Lord of your life, the offense will lead to a divide. Want to see how powerful offense is? It's so powerful, it limited Jesus' miracles. If you are not feeling the presence of God, check your offense.

> Isn't this the carpenter? Isn't this Mary's son and the brother of James, Joseph, Judas, and Simon? Aren't his sisters here with us?" And

they took offense at him. He could not do any
miracles there, except lay his hands on a few
sick people and heal them (Mark 6:3, 5).

This is important! Offense is so powerful; it blocks us from
receiving Jesus' miracles. If you are not feeling the presence
of Jesus, check your offense! The offense may be the sign of
an idol. If it is an idol, you may feel the need to rationalize or
justify it. Make no mistake about it, if you have an idol in your
life, Jesus will offend you. Just know that when He does, it is
for your own good. It's time to acknowledge and dethrone the
idols that get in the way of following Jesus.

Questions:

1. Take a moment to think about a time when you overreacted to an offense. Looking back, is it easy for you to
   justify your response? Why or why not?

2. Still thinking about that time you overreacted to an
   offense, if you could go back in time, how would you
   respond today?

3. How do you think Jesus would have responded to the
   thing that offended you?

4. How does following Jesus help us stop the natural desire
   to crucify those who offend us?

5. Based on this chapter, what is one thing that you are
   going to do?

CHAPTER 6

AREN'T CHRISTIANS SUPPOSED TO BE OFFENDED

"Being offended is inevitable. Living offended
is a choice." –Craig Groeschel

I've been a Christian for so long I can already anticipate the
pushback from the last chapter. There are many Christians
who think, "Aren't Christians supposed to get offended and call
out the world?" To some, following Jesus leads to being more
offended, not less.

The thought is, there is real evil in the world and we must
stand against it. That is true, but if your stance doesn't change
anything, does it really matter? So often outrage only focuses
on the immediate. We rant because we are offended, but we lose
site of the big picture of winning people over. Please hear me,
I'm not advocating for remaining silent in the face of injustice.
I think there is a way that is more beneficial than how we typically respond to offense. In this chapter, I aim to show why
Scripture, itself, offers a better way to handle offense.

Every passionate person with a cause finds a Bible verse to
try and support their view. Whenever I share about not getting
offended online, a Christian will quickly throw Bible verses at

me. The common idea is that there is anger in the Bible, so we are justified to get angry with injustice.

Just because someone did something in the Bible does not mean that we are supposed to follow in their example. Some of the Bible is prescriptive and some of it is descriptive. Prescriptive texts are the ones that tell us how to love God and love other people. The commands and principles that we find throughout Scripture are prescriptive. Some of those commands were for specific

> *The Bible is not about you. It's unhealthy to read yourself into every text.*

times and some of the commands are for all times. A lot of the Old Testament contains ceremonial and religious laws that Christians are not bound to follow. We can learn from those texts, but the context tells us that those commands are not for us. Context matters. Not everything in the Bible is a command for us to follow. Some of it is simply there for us to see what we should not do. The Bible is not about you. It's unhealthy to read yourself into every text. When we read ourselves into the text, we can miss what God is wanting to teach us.

Not only are there prescriptive texts, but there are also descriptive texts. The descriptive texts are the ones that simply tell the story of God's people. God's people come with flaws, issues, and massive sins. I love that the Bible didn't edit out all the flaws of those who follow God. The flaws are mentioned all throughout. The flaws are what I relate to the most. I can see myself in the people who love God but still have issues. You cannot find a perfect follower of God, outside of Jesus.

Just because there is a biblical example, doesn't mean we throw out wisdom and use that to justify our behaviors today.

It's the same thing with our offense and anger. There are examples in the Scriptures of people losing their cool after they got offended, but be careful using that as justification. There are lots of people who lose their cool in the Scriptures (descriptive), but there are no commands for us to become offended (prescriptive). Contrast that with the commands that we are given to bring unity, peace, and love. I believe you'll see God's ultimate plan is for us to bring peace to the chaos. The Scriptures share this idea multiple times.

COMMANDS FOR PEACE

"Blessed are the peacemakers, for they will be called children of God" (Matthew 5:9).

"For, whoever would love life and see good days must keep their tongue from evil and their lips from deceitful speech. They must turn from evil and do good; they must seek peace and pursue it" (1 Peter 3:10-11).

"Bear with each other and forgive one another if any of you has a grievance against someone. Forgive as the Lord forgave you" (Colossians 3:13).

"Let the peace of Christ rule in your hearts, since as members of one body you were called to peace. And be thankful" (Colossians 3:15).

"Peacemakers who sow in peace reap a harvest of righteousness" (James 3:18).

"Turn from evil and do good; seek peace and pursue it" (Psalm 34:14).

"Make every effort to live in peace with everyone and to be holy; without holiness no one will see the Lord" (Hebrews 12:14).

"It is to one's honor to avoid strife, but every fool is quick to quarrel" (Proverbs 20:3).

"Good sense makes one slow to anger, and it is his glory to overlook an offense" (Proverbs 19:11).

It's hard to ignore the commands to seek peace, be slow to anger, and forgive others. You can find examples to support almost any agenda you want. That is often what outsiders do. Christians, on the other hand, should understand how to read the Bible and submit their lives to the teaching of Scripture. If there is a command to be offended, I don't know about it. On the other hand, there are lots of commands and teachings on bringing peace, forgiving, and overlooking an offense. When we are following Jesus, He will lead us to reach across the aisle and form relationships with those who offend us. Mature Christians do something productive with their offense. Anyone can rant, yell, complain, boycott, or unfriend, but if we truly want to make a difference, we must do something different. Christian maturity is when you have the power to destroy someone who offended you, but instead you try to build a bridge to reach them. Simply yelling at the darkness doesn't turn on the lights. And that is the biggest problem with being offended. When we get offended, it hurts, and in that hurt, we lose sight of the big picture. We forget that we are representing Jesus. We forget that the person who offended us is one whom Jesus loves. We forget that the big picture is that we love and win over our enemies.

THIS SEEMS IMPOSSIBLY DIFFICULT

In 1953, Elisabeth married Jim Elliot. Soon after the wedding, they packed up their lives and moved to the mission field. They went to share the Gospel with the Aquas Indians in Ecuador. After initially finding a connection with the tribe, Jim Elliot and the other missionary men who were with him were brutally attacked and killed. Elisabeth was left with a newborn daughter and would have had

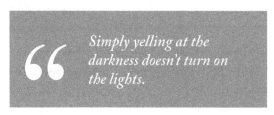

Simply yelling at the darkness doesn't turn on the lights.

every right to leave the mission field bitter and angry. Why didn't God protect her husband? Why weren't they blessed for trying to do God's work? What can we do to get back at the tribe who savagely killed her husband? Those are questions that I think most of us would ask. Instead, Elisabeth Elliot committed to reach out to the very people who killed her husband. In her book titled *Discipline* she wrote,

> "It is the will that must deal with the feelings. The will must triumph over them, but only the

will that is surrendered to Christ can do this."
–Elizabeth Elliot.

Only a will that is surrendered to Christ can do this. Only a will that is more committed to Jesus than personal offense can learn to forgive those who wrong it. Elizabeth could have easily chosen to be bitter and angry. Instead, she chose to value the life of the very people who attempted to ruin hers. Over the next two years, she was able to form a relationship with some women in the Aqua tribe and eventually learned their language. The Aqua people did not feel she was a threat, and because of her efforts, she was able to see the tribe receive Jesus. One of the first converts was one of the men who was responsible for attacking her husband and killing one of the other

> *Only a will that is more committed to Jesus than personal offense can learn to forgive those who wrong it.*

missionaries. He personally used his spear to kill one of the missionaries who was with Jim on that fateful day. The Gospel radically changed the tribe. So much so they changed their name. The name Aqua means "Savage" and they changed their name to Waorani which means "They are true people."

To follow Jesus is to have a new identity. We are no longer to act in our own savage nature. Instead, we are to respond with the love of Jesus. It's like what Pastor Chris Durso says, "Don't let your emotions or your offense override your theology." Our theology teaches us to forgive. Our theology teaches that we are new creations and we are to be separate from the world. It is only the love of Jesus that can lead us to reach out to someone who offends us. It is only the love of Jesus that can propel us to form a relationship with the very people who stand against us. I don't know about you, but I want to live that type of story— story where the power of God helps me to win over the very people who offend me.

KILL EM WITH KINDNESS

If you really want to get back at those who offend you, try killing them with kindness. In this day and age, that's a bold strategy. As a Christian, the way we respond to offense should be different than those without Jesus. The world fights back with protests, arguments, fighting, and canceling. We see the results that those things produce. It doesn't change anyone's mind, and it certainly doesn't make the

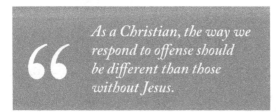

As a Christian, the way we respond to offense should be different than those without Jesus.

world a better place. As Christians, we are called to love the very people who offend us. We can do that by killing them with kindness.

I was first exposed to this idea in the ninth grade. My best friend, at the time, was loved by the ladies. He didn't go to my school, but because we were friends, he would come with me to basketball games. The girls really liked him. This didn't sit well with the other guys. One guy, in particular, made it clear that he did not like my friend. I'm pretty sure it had something to do with his girlfriend accidentally calling him by my friend's name. It also could have to do with the fact that his girlfriend wrote her first name with my friend's last name all over the inside of her book covers. The boyfriend made it abundantly clear that he wanted to introduce my incredibly good-looking friend's face to his fist. Now, for the most part, because they went to different schools, and because we didn't have social media, it was easy for them to avoid each other. That all changed when my school hosted a community wide basketball tournament. The coach who picked the team didn't know about all the drama between my insanely good-looking friend and the guy with a girlfriend. The coach asked both of them to be on the team. When I saw the roster, I immediately went to my friend with the looks of a Greek god, and told him the news. I asked what he was going to do and he said, "I'm going to put hot coals on his head." I wasn't familiar with that tactic. I had so many questions. Where are these coals going to come from? Are we going to pelt them at the boyfriend from a safe distance? He quickly explained that he was going to kill him with kindness. He shared the following verse with me:

> If your enemy is hungry, give him food to eat; And if he is thirsty, give him water to drink; For you will heap burning coals on his head, And the Lord will reward you (Proverbs 25:21-22).

That's a bold strategy. Instead of fighting, boycotting, or trying to hurt others the way they hurt you, the people of God are called to be kind to their enemies. When the tournament came around, my friend with the face of an angel went above and beyond to show kindness to the disgruntled boyfriend. He passed him the ball...a lot. He encouraged him when he made a shot. At first, he got the cold shoulder, but by the end of the first game they were friends. It's a friendship that continues to this day. Neither of them ended up with the girl who was the center of the drama, but both of them ended up being friends. It doesn't take strength to be mean. It doesn't take strength to gossip or tear others down. That is easy. It takes supernatural strength to be kind to someone who doesn't like you.

The way you kill someone with kindness is by showing your enemies kindness. In the verse above, the word enemy is literally translated to mean "Those who hate you". Haters are going to hate, and people who love God are going to show them kindness.

Tell me that's weakness. I don't think you can. Try it. It takes so much strength to be kind to those with whom you disagree. We all could use a lot more killing with kindness.

You see, you can find examples in the Bible of people getting angry. You can find examples of people reacting to that anger. Yet, you cannot find a verse that tells a Christian to live offended. Instead, there are lots of verses that call us to die to ourselves, serve our enemies, and respond to offense with love. I know it's a bold strategy, but it's the very thing God uses to change the world.

Questions:

1. Before reading this chapter, did you believe Christians were called to be offended? Why or why not?

2. How can you take a stand against injustice while not standing against people?

3. Who is someone you disagree with today? What can you do to remember to pray for them?

4. Based on this chapter, what is one thing you are going to take away?

PART II

This is where I hope to get really practical. I've mentioned this multiple times, but it is not enough to be offended. I challenge every person reading this, and especially every Christian, to look at the results of their offense. If your offense is helping people fall in love with Jesus, helping you love other people, and making a difference in the world, then keep doing what you are doing. If it's not, then why not try another strategy? That strategy is what I will lay out in the next few chapters. Often, when we get offended, we place the offense over the relationship. Family members have stopped talking, friendships have ended, and church members have left with church hurt because of an offense. Because offense is a hurt it can be easy to put the hurt over the relationship. Because of Jesus, Christians should have the most forgiving, grace filled, and healthy relationships. The following sections will help us take the focus off our hurt and onto the relationship. I believe the way forward is through influence, friendship, and hospitality. Let's start with influence.

CHAPTER 7

INFLUENCE

"As a Christian, my mantra is not to win an argument, but to win people." – Edwin Jones

I want to share something with which you will probably disagree. Most people I know disagree with this, but I do it anyway. Here it is...you ready? I choose not to block, hide, or unfriend people on social media. I hear all the time that people do it for their own sanity. I get it. Social media can be maddening. At the same time, I think it points to how easily we are offended by different ideas. This is where humility enters. I see people unfollow people all the time because they disagree with an opinion. Why are we so offended by a different opinion?

It's not easy. In fact, life would be easier if I did block and unfriend people. Especially during political season! I choose to stay in relationship with people I disagree with for one reason... influence. I want to challenge you to do the same thing.

I don't love drama, and yet social media has provided a lot of drama for me. It seems like someone is always upset, and everyone wants me to take sides. The following is a real-life anonymous letter I received. I got it after my kids and I started playing the video game, Fortnite, together. I posted a pic on Instagram and within a few days I received this letter:

> "Should you as a pastor play Fortnite? Site said
> not suitable for persons under 12 due to violence.
> Video gaming is addictive. Maybe a sermon."

A few thoughts about that letter. First, Christians who feel they have some coaching or correction to share, should also have the guts to say it in person. Anonymous letters are for cowards. They lack the opportunity to hear another perspective and they lack the credibility to truly influence change. Second, that letter didn't stop me from playing

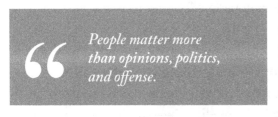

People matter more than opinions, politics, and offense.

Fortnite. It did make me feel like I was being judged for what I posted online. That type of judgment can lead a person to want to be fake online. I aim to be authentic, so what you see is what you get. The person made me feel judged but didn't inspire me to change. The person who wrote that letter might be 100% right, but their approach is 100% wrong! This person didn't influence me to change because they have zero influence in my life. I don't know who they are! I believe they were trying to help, but they didn't.

I think way too often people get focused on an issue in front of them and forget the big picture. The big picture is that people matter! People matter more than opinions, politics, and offense. I believe that when we follow Jesus, it sets us up to become influential. The influence is not done by might, power, or fighting. It's done by living for Jesus, who in turn leads us to care for those who disagree with us.

The big picture is that we are called to influence people and change the world. So, what is influence? Great question! Thank you for asking it!

Influence is the capacity to have an impact on someone.[4]

Whether it's positive or negative, each of us has the capacity to impact someone. When we avoid people with whom we disagree, and when we are quick to unfollow people we know because of a different opinion, we lose the chance to have influence. At the same time, we also create an echo chamber where we only hear from people with whom we agree. You have the ability to influence people, but it's tough to do when you block, avoid, and unfriend those who disagree with you.

I HAVE INFLUENCE?

For years I blogged five days a week at robshep.com. It was a little blog that, in the grand scheme of things, was considered mid-size. I was happy with my following. I had, on average, a thousand people a day read my blog, but compared to the big wigs I was small time. I never thought about the fact that I had influence. I just posted my thoughts and tried to make people laugh and think.

So, one time I went to a Christian conference in Atlanta, and I wrote a blog post featuring my thoughts on said conference. A very small part of the post included a throw away com ment: "If I was single, I would move to Atlanta because there are a lot of single Christians". It was such a small part of the

---

[4] Oxford English Dictionary

post that I forgot I wrote it. Two years later, a friend posted on Facebook about her wedding. She shared in her post that she moved to Atlanta because she once read a post where I mentioned that if I was single that's where I'd go. Are you joking me? That's crazy! I didn't know I had that type of influence! I had no idea she read my blog. As you are reading that, I bet there is some memory coming to you. It may not be a marriage, but I bet you've influenced someone to do something. Even if it was to trying a new restaurant, reading a book, or watching a new TV show, you've influenced someone.

I believe that you and I have more influence than we realize. It may not be until Heaven when we realize the impact that we truly had. It could have been a kind gesture at a restaurant, an encouraging text you sent, teaching kids at church, showing up to support a friend, or even simply being consistent with your walk with God. All it takes to have influence is the capacity to have an impact on someone. You have that capacity. The question is, will you use it to impact someone for Jesus?

Everyone has some influence. If you don't have a lot, you can always gain more. Influence is something that is gained incrementally, but lost instantly.

Whether you care about influence or not, if you are a Christian, you are called to influence people. I'll show you this in the next section. Being a light in the world is a way to influence others. Whether it's your friends, kids, your spouse, or coworkers, we all have the potential to influence someone. I want to show you why this is so important for Christians. The Apostle Paul gives us some insight on how to be an influential Chriotian.

BECOME ALL THINGS TO ALL

In Paul's day, the issue wasn't Republican vs. Democrat. It was Jew vs. Gentile. The church was made up of Jewish Christians and also Gentiles who converted to Christianity. These two groups didn't like one another and often fought. In fact, there was a time when Paul calls out Jesus' disciple, Peter, because he was excluding the Gentiles. I tell you that just to say there was a lot of division. With that context, let's look at what Paul says:

> "Though I am free and belong to no one, I have made myself a slave to everyone, to win as many as possible" (1 Corinthians 9:19).

This is strong language. Slavery in Paul's day was different than the slavery we learn about in American history. In Paul's day, a slave was more of an indentured servant. You weren't a slave because of race, but because of a debt that was owed. Meaning, you could earn your way out of slavery. Even with it being a different system...it's still slavery. No one chooses to be a slave. As humans we crave freedom. When Paul says he made himself a slave to everyone, he is saying this is his choice. Paul makes it clear that he doesn't have to belong to either group. He was born Jewish, but he is also the leader of the Gentile converts. He has one foot in each camp, and people didn't like it. Paul says that he makes himself a slave to everyone to win as many as possible. What does that mean? Great question, I'm glad you asked. Let's keep reading the text:

> To the Jews I became like a Jew, to win the Jews.
> To those under the law I became like one under
> the law (though I myself am not under the law),
> so as to win those under the law. To those not
> having the law I became like one not having the
> law (though I am not free from God's law but
> am under Christ's law), so as to win those not
> having the law. To the weak I became weak, to
> win the weak. (1 Corinthians 9:20-21).

Okay, this is HUGE! Paul's ultimate goal is to win people to Jesus! He does that by meeting them where they are. That's influence! So, Paul finds out what he has in common with both groups of people and then focuses on that. That's not how most people act today. Over and over again, I see this mantra playing out. If you are not with me, you are my enemy. You know who famously said that? Anakin Skywalker on his way to becoming Darth Vader. I know it's fiction, but Darth's way of getting

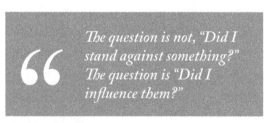

The question is not, "Did I stand against something?" The question is "Did I influence them?"

along with people is to force everyone to agree with him, and if they don't, he pinches his fin-gers together and uses the force to choke them to death. That's the dark side! After Anakin says that, his mentor, Obi Wan, says, "Only a Sith deals in absolutes." In case you hate all things Star Wars, the point is that only the dark side speaks in absolutes. Only the dark side desires to go to war with those who disagree. I know it is "A long time ago, in a galaxy far, far, away." However, way before Obi Wan said this, the Apostle Paul gave the same idea. Christians are called to win over those who disagree, but we don't do it with force. We do it with influence and love. Paul did what he could to relate to both groups so that he could influence both groups to fall in love with Jesus! Influence is the key to this. We win people by influence, not arguments!

The question is not, "Did I stand against something?" The question is "Did I influence them?" You have the potential to influence people. You may be a truth teller. That is, you are someone who says what you think no matter how it impacts others. If you tell someone the truth, you probably feel better because you did what felt right to you. At the same time, I think you have probably become frustrated because others didn't respond to your truth. I don't want you to stop telling the truth. We need you! I just hope to influence you to tell the truth in a way that has positive influence. You do this by showing support, love, and kindness, even more than your truth telling. It is difficult to hear the hard truth when there is not much love and support to go with it.

When you are trying to influence people you have to speak to them in a way that they will be receptive to. Even if they are not receptive, you must learn to speak to them in a way that will be received. Otherwise we end up arguing, yelling, ranting, and changing nothing. Often in our passion for our cause we end up yelling at the other side. When this happens they don't listen. I know this is true because you don't listen when the other side yells at you. Christians need to do a better job of speaking in a way that will be received well by those who disagree with them. The Apostle Paul says,

> I have become all things to all people so that
> by all possible means I might save some. I do
> all this for the sake of the gospel, that I may
> share in its blessings, and belong to no one, I
> have made myself a slave to everyone, to win as
> many as possible (1 Corinthians 9:22-23).

Let's just zoom out for a second. Did Paul have influence? He wrote over half of the New Testament! How did he gain influence? He became all things to all people so that he could win as many as possible! Paul told the truth. He wasn't afraid to confront someone. At the same time, he worked hard at remembering the big picture. The big picture was not simply to confront, but to influence change—specifically, to influence people to accept Jesus.

Arguing and debating doesn't gain influence towards those we are trying to influence. In fact, it loses it. Have you ever changed your mind because someone yelled at you on social media? We lose that potential when we see those we disagree with as the enemy. This is why, as a Christian, the goal is to win people, not arguments. We must learn what others love in order to win them over. Paul became all things to all people in order to win some for Jesus. It's the difference between playing the long game and the short game. The short game is focused on the immediate, so if someone is wrong you must correct them right away. That is true for life threatening events, but not so much with ideas. All of us have had multiple crazy ideas throughout the years. The long game focuses on keeping the relationship in order to have influence. I have a friend who cut off all ties to his cousin because his cousin became a progressive Christian. He was so hurt and upset with his cousin that he cut him out of his life. That is a natural reaction to offense. He was hurt so he reacted, but that is the short game. In the long run it's better to try to keep the relationship in order to influence him. He may have to set up some boundaries, the relationship may look different, but he still leaves the door open to influence his cousin.

HOW DO WE DO THIS?

Practically speaking, how do we influence others? In a world that is so divided and people are so focused on what they are against, how do we become all things to all people so that we might win some? The answer is to follow in Paul's example. Paul knew what he believed, and at the same time he accommodated those who did not agree with him. Accommodate means to adjust to someone else's needs.[5]

Relationships are so incredibly difficult because we don't like to accommodate. That's why keeping an eye on the mission is so important. You may not want to make an accommodation but if it will help someone else meet Jesus, you should.

A BIBLICAL EXAMPLE

We actually have an example of Paul accommodating others in the Scriptures. The Apostle Paul was a missionary and often went to places that were pagan. When he was in Athens, he was troubled because of all the pagan worship. The Scriptures say he was, "greatly distressed." Paul was triggered. So, what does Paul do with his offense? He goes to where the people are and teaches about Jesus. Look at how he starts his

---

[5] Oxford English Dictionary

conversation with the very people who worshipped the idols that offended him,

> People of Athens! I see that in every way you are very religious. For as I walked around and looked carefully at your objects of worship, I even found an altar with this inscription: to an unknown god (Acts 17:22-23).

Did you catch what Paul did? He starts with where the people of Athens were; they were very religious. In order to know that, he had to look very carefully. If he stopped at the city entrance and let his offense stop him, he would have never seen an altar to an unknown god. He then pulls a brilliant move and tells the people of Athens who that unknown God is. He flips the script and tells them that the unknown god they worship is the real God, Jesus.

Now, Paul didn't win over everyone. Some people thought he was crazy. Some listened for a while, but then left. Some were won over and became followers of Jesus. Paul says he becomes all things to all people to win some. He knows that not everyone will be won over. Paul did this by starting with common ground. He didn't announce that he was against pagan worship. He didn't point out how silly the people of Athens were for believing in gods that don't exist. He didn't post a meme that shamed the people of Athens. Paul had to work hard to find common ground with those he disagreed with. Why would he do that?

"I do all this for the sake of the gospel" – Paul

Paul's ultimate goal is to accommodate people in a way that helps them become receptive to the gospel. That gospel is the message of Jesus. We are broken sinners, but Jesus came to die for sinners like you and me. We are far more sinful than we would care to admit, but way more loved than we could ever imagine. That's the gospel. It's the foundation of Christianity. We accommodate others by finding common ground and then showing them how the gospel changes everything. In order to do this we have to actually know some lost people. We can't wait for the lost to wander into our churches. We need to get proactive and beg God for opportunities to share the Gospel with others. I love the quote from Joseph C. Aldrich,

> "We're not called to shout the good news from a safe and respectable distance and then leave. To reach men and women for Christ, we must voluntarily lay aside the temptation to be detached from the unsaved or to lord it over them."[6]

We saw the Apostle Paul do that very thing. He wasn't detached from the lost. He went to where they were. He didn't yell at them from the safety of a computer screen. He met them where they were at and found a way to accommodate them. We should follow Paul's example!

It doesn't mean the message changes. It means the methods that we use change in order to meet the needs of other people.

I love what author Dale Carnegie says,

---

[6] From Gentle Persuasion: Creative Ways to Introduce Your Friends to Christ by Joseph C. Aldrich

"Personally, I am very fond of strawberries and cream, but I have found that for some strange reason, fish prefer worms. So, when I went fishing, I didn't think about what I wanted. I thought about what they wanted. I didn't bait the hook with strawberries and cream. Rather, I dangled a worm or grasshopper in front of the fish and said:

'Wouldn't you like to have that?' Why not use the same common sense when fishing for people?"
— *How to Win Friends and Influence People*

This is how we become all things to all people. We stick to truth, but we adjust our strategy based on the audience. Jesus wants us to fish for people. The bait that we use is a supernatural love that isn't dependent on how the fish treat us. It's based on how we have been treated by God. You have influence. The question is, are you using that influence to point people back to Jesus? So often Christians want others to accommodate them, while they aren't very accommodating of others.

PROSTITUTES AND THE GOSPEL

Author Tony Campolo shares an amazing story of a time he accommodated a prostitute. I know that is a shocking thing to read, but reserve your judgment until after the story.

One night after a long night of ministry, Tony Campolo sat by himself in a dirty diner. It was the type of place that had greasy food and questionable cleaning methods. While he was eating, he saw a group of prostitutes come into the restaurant.

They were just getting off work and he couldn't help but overhear their conversation. One of them, named Agnus, shared that tomorrow was her birthday. She was quickly met with ridicule. The other women didn't care it was her birthday and reminded her that no one else would care. At that moment, Tony got an idea. He walked up to one of the employees, Harry, and asked about Agnus. He was told that she and her fellow ladies

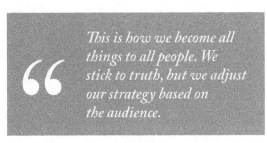

This is how we become all things to all people. We stick to truth, but we adjust our strategy based on the audience.

of the night come into that restaurant every night after working hours. Tony pitched the idea to throw her a birthday party, and that's exactly what he did.

The next night, he got there early enough to decorate. He provided a cake and birthday decorations. The whole restaurant ended up getting in on this to surprise Agnus. When Agnus walked in, she was completely shocked. In a surprising move, after seeing the cake, she quickly asked if she could take the cake home. She shared that she had never had a cake of her own and wanted to save it. She rushed home and promised to come right back to the party. At that moment, Tony didn't know what else to do. The birthday girl was gone and he was standing around with a bunch of strangers who had just thrown a party for a prostitute. Tony did what came natural to him and asked if they could pray. Imagine asking this group to pray. I would feel so nervous, but this group willingly went along as Tony prayed for Agnus. As soon as he said, "Amen", Harry leaned over the counter and with a trace of hostility in his voice, he said, "Hey! You never told me you were a preacher. What kind of church do you belong to?" In one of those moments when just the right words came, Tony answered, "I belong to a church that throws birthday parties for whores at 3:30 in the morning." Harry waited a moment and then almost sneered as he answered, "No you don't. There's no church like that. If there was, I'd join it. I'd join a church like that!"

Wouldn't it be amazing to be a part of a church like that? Well, that's the kind of church that Jesus came to create! If you currently aren't at a church like that, then you can help it become one. Don't wait for the pastor or church staff to start fishing for people. The church is not a building, it's people. When you accommodate others, share the love of Jesus in practical ways with those with whom you disagree, and show kindness to those who don't deserve it; you are being the church of Jesus. In order to influence people with whom you disagree, you are going to have to change your perspective. I'll cover that in the next chapter.

Questions:

1. Who has the biggest influence over your life?

2. How have you seen your influence impact someone else?

3. A Christian's goal is to win people, not arguments. Do you agree or disagree with that quote?

4. If a Christian's goal is to win people, how can we gain that influence?

CHAPTER 8

How To Be Known For What You Are For

> "In a hyper-cynical world that is often known for what it's against, let's be a group of people known for who and what we're for."
> –Jeff Henderson

The first way to gain influence is to accommodate others. Again, that does not mean that we don't stand for what we believe. We maintain core values. It simply means that we have the humility to understand others. In order to reach people, we must think through our approach. The next step is to become known for what you are for instead of what you are against.

Ranting about someone's sin doesn't stop people from sinning.

HOW TO BE KNOWN FOR WHAT YOU ARE FOR!

To be known for what you are for instead of what you are against, you must commit to focus on what you are going to do or are doing to fix a problem. Ranting about someone's sin doesn't stop people from sinning. Ranting against politics rarely convinces anyone to change their vote. When Christians complain, boycott, and rant online but offer no alternatives, the world rolls its eyes, and then moves on. It is only when we offer a more excellent way that we have a chance to gain influence. The key is to show people what you are for and continually share your why.

Think about it this way. When someone tells you that something you like is horrible, you don't respond well. In fact, telling people what they love is wrong leads them to double down on their stance. Instead, let's offer a better picture! It looks like this. Compare option 1 with option 2 and notice the difference.

Option 1:

Dwight–Fact: Rob Shepherd is a heretic and people who listen to him preach just want their ears to be tickled.

Option 2:

Jim–I love listening to sound theology! It's important to understand what the Bible says. We better understand the Bible when we understand the context, history, and original intent.

The first option may be true, but it will not convince anyone to change their opinion. Instead, it will cause people to double down. The second option shares what Jim is for. Jim is painting a picture of what he thinks is true without tearing down what he is against. He is teaching people instead of ranting against people. With option one the people who already agree with Dwight will jump on board and hurl insults at Pastor Rob's preaching. Those that disagree will either ignore it or end up in an argument. It is highly unlikely that with the first option anyone's mind will be changed.

The early church has an example of how to be known for what you are for. During the early days of Christianity in Rome, the common practice was infanticide. It was believed that it was good for society. So, if you had a baby with special needs or a deformity or if a family had too many girls, it was encouraged to get rid of the baby. The way they would dispose of the baby was to take a baby to the woods outside of the city and leave it there. They would let the gods or fate decide. This was a way for them to get rid of their unwanted baby and also not feel guilty about it because they left it in the god's hands. Christians from the very beginning condemned this practice. They didn't condemn it with Facebook rants, boycotts, or fighting. They condemned this practice and then did something about it. The early Christians would intentionally go into the woods to look for babies that were left to die. When they found a baby, they would take the baby into their own homes and raise it as their own. It was the Christian's belief that every human is a life created in the image of God that led them to rescue and care for babies. In 318 AD, Emperor Constantine declares that infanticide is illegal. Constantine did this because Christians forbid infanticide. We literally have an example of Christians changing culture and laws that impacted the lives of babies.

The change came from action. They didn't wait for the law to change to do something about the infanticide in their world.

Our words are important, but our actions are the fuel that give our words movement. What if Christians today followed the example of the early church? What if we became so known for taking care of babies that every woman in the world knew she had another option instead of abortion? What if Christians took such good care of people that women felt safe enough to share about an unwanted pregnancy? What if anyone who had an unwanted pregnancy didn't have to be afraid? What if they knew that their financial needs would be met? What if they knew someone would be there with them through every step of the process. What if they knew that there was another option?

The Roman government and eventually the world was changed by the love of Christians. Aristides was a second-century philosopher. He was also a pagan, who admired the followers of Jesus and defended them in a letter addressed to Emperor Hadrian. Pay attention to how Aristides described the Christians to the Roman Emperor Hadrian:

> The Christians love one another. They never fail
> to help widows; they save orphans from those
> who would hurt them. If a man has something,
> he gives freely to the man who has nothing. If
> they see a stranger, Christians take him home
> and are happy, as though he were a real brother.
> They don't consider themselves brothers in the
> usual sense, but brothers instead through the
> Spirit of God. And if they hear that one of them
> is in jail, or persecuted for professing the name
> of their redeemer, they all give him what he

needs. If it is possible, they bail him out. If one of them is poor and there isn't enough food to go around, they fast several days to give him the food he needs. This is really a new kind of person. There is something divine in them.

–Aristides[7]

That is powerful! That is how we become known for what we are for. Make no mistake the early Christians were persecuted. What changed the world's perspective of them was how they loved one another.

To be known for what you are for will still get you some criticism. Paul got lots of criticism, and people even tried to kill him on multiple occasions. Not everyone who listened to Paul's message repented. He did this though to win some. I'm convinced that yelling and screaming about how wrong

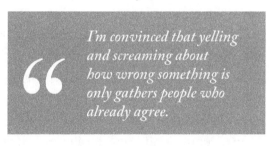

I'm convinced that yelling and screaming about how wrong something is only gathers people who already agree.

something is only gathers people who already agree. If we want to win some, we have to figure out another way. That DOES NOT MEAN WE DON'T TAKE A STAND! Being what you are for is a stand. As the band, Jars of Clay, once sang, "Love is the protest."[8]

---

[7] http://www.earlychristianwritings.com/text/aristides-kay.html

[8] Jars of Clay. "Love is the Protest" Jars of Clay: Greatest Hits. Provident Label Group LLC, 2008. CD.

It's a stand to not add to the negativity. It's a stand to try and win some. What if the church in America was the safest place for people who had an unplanned pregnancy? Do these women know they are welcomed in the church? We have all done things we regret and the church should be the safest place in the world for those with regret.

One of Jesus' best friends, Peter, wrote this to the church, "Live such good lives among the pagans that, though they accuse you of doing wrong, they may see your good deeds and glorify God on the day he visits us." (1 Peter 2:12).

In life someone will always be critical. Even if you were perfect, someone would crucify you. That's a great title for a book! The point is that no matter what you do someone will crucify you. However, that doesn't mean that you intentionally try to tick off people with whom you disagree. The goal is not to simply gather people who already agree with us. The goal is also not to destroy those who disagree with us. The goal is to influence and impact those who do not believe as we do.

> "Any fool can criticize, complain, and con-
> demn—and most fools do. But it takes char-
> acter and self-control to be understanding and
> forgiving."–Dale Carnegie from *How to Win
> Friends and Influence People.*

Any fool can criticize! Christians should be different! Sure, there are lots of things to complain about, but let's be so busy changing the world that we don't have time to complain!

As Christians, our goal should be to live such good lives that even when others accuse us of doing wrong, they see our good deeds. The church hasn't been living this way for some time, and it shows.

Be known for adoption because you are for life. Be known for generosity because you know the damage of greed. Be known for making a difference in the world in the name of Jesus. Be known for unity because we are called to reconciliation because Jesus first reconciled us. Be known for grace because every saint is a sinner. Be known for showing love to those you disagree with. Be known for what we are for and not all the things we are against.

I'm so passionate about this message because I continue to see the church lose influence in America. As of this writing, for the first time in 100 years, less than 50 percent of Americans claim membership to a church. There are 2.7 million people who become inactive every year from American churches. At the same time, 2.7 million people convert to Christianity around the world. That is not sustainable. It's not sustainable to lose as many as we gain around the world. Scandals, infighting, and declaring war on culture has had an impact on the influence of Christians in the world. If you are reading this, you can be part of the change. Let's commit to be known for what we are for more than what we are against.

The best way to stop the spread of evil is to replace it with something good. This is redeeming culture. If you are tired of smut on television then invest in companies that are trying to make clean content. If you can't make movies, invest in those who can. If you are tired of negativity on social media, commit to share inspiring messages of hope every day. Dream big. What can you do to redeem culture? We have a lot of preachers and teachers. We need more every day Christians to live out their faith in a way that makes the world take notice.

A REAL LIFE EXAMPLE

My friends Randall and Kelley Nichols experienced, first hand, the difficulties of adopting and fostering. They live out what they are for, and it is inspiring. They adopted two girls, both with special needs. With three kids, and full-time work on a church staff, their plates were already full. Their experiences, however, led to some frustrations. Adopting can feel lonely, is expensive, and can be a long emotional process. The Nichols experienced that. At the same time, with twenty years of church staff experience, they saw the frustration of pastors trying to mobilize people to make a difference. There are lots of needs, and those needs can feel overwhelming. The overwhelming feeling can lead to inaction. From their perspective, it seemed as if the local church was not doing much of anything to support adoption. Randall and Kelley became triggered. It would have been easy to talk about all the issues with fostering and adopting. It would have been easy for them to blast the churches that seemed to not care about the widows and orphans of the world. It also would have been easy for them to give up and say, "No one else cares, so why should we?" Instead, they made a very difficult decision to do something positive. They made the extremely difficult decision to leave their jobs and start a brand new organization that bridges the gap between the church and the foster care system. There are lots of Christians who have the resources to help, but they lack a plan. That's where Randall and Kelley come in. They started "We Are The Echo" as a bridge to help churches and businesses come together to help end the foster care crisis in America. That's what I'm talking about! You don't have to choose between being passionate about changing the world or doing nothing. You can do something productive with what offends you in order to change the world. That's what Randall and Kelley have done, and it's full of awesome! To learn more about We Are the Echo visit their website wearetheecho.org.

It's people like Randall and Kelly who are known for what they are for. I bet if you asked them, they would admit to having some issues with various things in this world. They don't make that known because they are too busy sharing what they are for. I believe when Christians focus on what they are ultimately for, it leads them to have greater influence in the world. This is how we become known for what we are for.

Questions:

1. What was your biggest takeaway from this chapter?

2. What are some issues you see in the world?

3. Which issue are you most passionate about?

4. Even if it's once a month, what is something you can do to intentionally make a difference with the issue you are most passionate about?

CHAPTER 9

REDEEM CULTURE

"Christians do not condone unbiblical living; we redeem it." – Mike Yaconelli

There is a culture war going on in America. It's been going on for some time. It's not just the right vs. the left, it's also Christians vs. non-Christians. Not everyone participates in this battle. Many do, but many also seem to bury their heads in the sand. It seems like the only two options are to fight or avoid. There is a third option that I don't see shared a lot. I believe it's the option Jesus gives us.

Let me ask you a question. Are the people you adamantly disagree with enemies to fight against or opportunities to influence? Depending on how you answer that question will dictate how you feel about this chapter. If you feel like the problem is other people, and we need to avoid or fight against them, I'd like to offer you another option. I recently met with a pastor who was passionate about reaching his

> *Are the people you adamantly disagree with enemies to fight against or opportunities to influence?*

community for Jesus. He discovered a great resource to reach people. It was a system to gather prayer requests online. It has the potential to reach hundreds of people and simply pray for them. The catch is, the system uses Facebook and social media to find people. When this pastor went to his board, they immediately shut it down because, "The liberal media owns social media, and we shouldn't have anything to do with it." This pastor was crushed.

In order to influence others, we need to change our perspective about them. When we feel offended, we easily turn the other person into an enemy. When this happens, we want to fight against them. Jesus' strategy is to love our enemies. Christians have a hard time doing that because

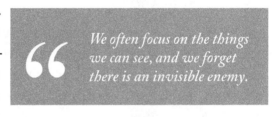

We often focus on the things we can see, and we forget there is an invisible enemy.

we so often focus on fighting a cultural war.

WE ARE FIGHTING THE WRONG WAR

In the Apostle Paul's day, there was a lot of offense and conflict. The culture fought against the Christians by persecuting them. Other religions fought against the Christians by trying to destroy the work they were doing, and there was a racial war going on between Jews and Gentiles. Amidst all of that turmoil, the Apostle Paul writes,

> "For we are not fighting against flesh-and-blood
> enemies, but against evil rulers and authorities
> of the unseen world" (Ephesians 6:12, NLT).

Our enemy is not other people. We often focus on the things we can see, and we forget there is an invisible enemy. This enemy knows the power of unity. You ever notice how there are zero Bible verses that reference Satan and his demons fighting with each other? They are always in unison. I believe that is why one of his favorite strategies is to get Christians fighting with each other. And, what is his favorite weapon of choice? Offense! The Devil separates us one offense at a time.

So often we focus on the things we can see, like other people, but the real war is something we cannot see. Behind every offense is a strategic plot to divide us. Yes, there are real problems in the world, and yes, there are evil people. They are real today, and they were very real in Paul's day. Paul, however, has an eternal perspective and challenges us to focus on the right war. My friend, Matt, says it like this:

> "We who often fuss and complain about the world would do well to remember that Jesus came because 'God so loved' it."–Matt Cannon

Remembering that we are in a spiritual war helps us not want to destroy other humans. Even when they are offensive, our goal should be to pray for them in order to see God redeem them. The goal is not to destroy them!

It is really important for Christians to wrestle with this. On the other side of your offense is someone God loves. Jesus didn't die for you because you are always right. You have been offensive towards God, yet God pursues a relationship with you! As Christians, we are called to show that same radical grace toward others.

At the end of the day, what result are we looking for with our offense? In your anger against an injustice, are you hoping the other side perishes or repents? Being a Christian is being a part of a redemptive movement. If our ultimate goal is to see people change, we cannot use the same methods as everyone else. I believe, as Christians, we have to offer something different than cancellation. We have to offer redemption.

REDEEM CULTURE

If yelling and screaming about what's wrong with the world doesn't change it, then we have to look closely at our actions. Instead of going to war, I believe Christians are called to redeem what is broken. I love the quote by author Mike Yaconelli...

> "Christians do not condone unbiblical living; we redeem it." – Mike Yaconelli

I've shared this quote with many Christians and they often struggle with it. Way too many have grown up hearing sermon after sermon about how we are to condemn the world. Therefore, they can't fathom another option. To redeem means to reclaim or repossess. Christians have been redeemed by Christ. That means our sin separated us from God, but because of Jesus' sacrifice, we are redeemed to God. We have full access to God (despite our sin) because of the forgiveness offered to us through Jesus. Redeemed people are called to redeem people.

So, what are some ways we redeem culture? For starters, we have to do something different than culture. Our culture has a boycott mentality. We live in a cancel culture society. If we truly want to change the world, we have to offer something different. This is where redemption applies.

EXAMPLES OF REDEEMING CULTURE

I grew up listening to the band dc Talk. They were my absolute favorite band. I read every article they were in, bought every album, and went to see them in concert multiple times—thirteen times to be exact. I may or may not have a scrap book in which I have kept all the articles, pictures, etc. My wife jokes on me for that one. I write all of that so you can understand I was a massive fan. One of the lyrics that stood out and helped shape my world view is, "If it's Christian, it ought to be better." The band, dc Talk attempted something few Christian artists have ever attempted. They did not sacrifice the quality of music, but at the same time, they boldly sang about Jesus. I remember watching their video for Jesus Freak on MTV's Headbangers Ball. This was back in the day when MTV played music videos. At the time, there were some Christians who were offended that dc Talk was on MTV. I didn't understand that offense. A song called Jesus Freak didn't have a place on MTV in the 90s, and yet the quality was so good it made others take notice. Back then, if a Christian artist wanted to go mainstream, they had to sacrifice the message. We saw other artists write love songs so vague you couldn't tell if it was to Jesus or a human. Some Christian artists abandon mentioning Jesus all together, but not dc Talk. The video for Jesus Freak was directed by Simon Maxwell, who also directed videos for the secular group Nine Inch Nails. This also caused some Christians to have a hissy fit. They declared that Christians should have nothing to do with the lost. They were convinced that dc Talk was of the devil. In my opinion, what dc Talk did is a perfect example of redeeming culture. They didn't change their message to work with others. They had non-Christians working for them. That's pretty impressive.

There are other ways to redeem culture. Halloween is a perfect example of this. I grew up in a day when Christians boycotted Halloween. It was seen as the Devil's holiday. My church hosted a harvest festival even though we weren't harvesting anything. The harvest festival was a chance for kids to dress up in costumes of Biblical heroes. We would still get candy, so the only difference was,

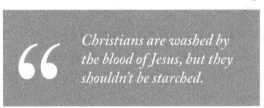

Christians are washed by the blood of Jesus, but they shouldn't be starched.

our costumes were based on people in the Bible. I used to joke about what the church would do if someone showed up as Adam or Eve wearing nothing but a fig leaf. The biggest hits every year were the kids who dressed up like the pastor. In some ways, it was memorable and fun, but it also was a missed opportunity to reach our neighbors.

Instead of boycotting what the Devil has, I'd like to offer a different perspective. The Devil has been stealing things that God created since the beginning of time. Sex is God's idea and the Devil finds a way to pervert it. Music is God's idea but the Devil finds ways to distort it. Even having a party is God's idea. There are commands to have celebrations all throughout the Bible. In my opinion, the world should be coming to Christians to find out how to have a good time. Christians are washed by the blood of Jesus, but they shouldn't be starched. Meaning, Christians should be the best at celebrating. We can laugh, have a good time, and celebrate in a way that honors God. We believe Jesus died and three days later rose from the grave. That's something to get excited about! So many of the parties today are vehicles to escape life. The Christian life is a way to live a life that doesn't need to escape. We should throw the best parties around. Listen, if the Devil has stolen something, I say we take it back! When it comes to Halloween, why should the Devil have all the good candy? If Halloween is the Devil's holiday, then let's redeem it. Halloween is one of the few times when my neighbors interact with one another. I want to take advantage of that. I do so by taking my kids Trick or Treating. They wear regular costumes, not Bible character costumes. I am their pastor, and I would be honored if they dressed like me, but so far neither of them has had any interest. If you want to dress your kid up like John the Baptist, I won't stand in your way, but I don't think that's the only way to redeem Halloween. It's the one time of year when we can engage our neighbors. I believe Halloween is a great time to go out and get to know someone who lives near you. Make a friend. For teenagers and adults in our culture, Halloween is a time when people can dress up slutty. It seems like every profession has a slutty costume version. Slutty nurse, slutty plumber, slutty police officer, slutty nun are all options of costumes in the section for adults. One way we redeem Halloween is by having fun without going slutty. We can stand out in culture without compromising our convictions. My point is, there are other ways to stand out besides boycotting. Why would I boycott the one time when my neighbors interact with me and my family?

We have created a culture that separates the sacred from the secular. Without a doubt, there should be some separations, but there should also be a lot of redeeming. There are limits to what we can redeem. I don't think we can redeem pornography.

Christian pornography cannot and should not exist. We don't redeem something by tagging Jesus on to it. We redeem something by transforming it in a way that honors God.

One time, I had a woman share how offended she was that a local church took over what used to be an ABC store. I failed to see the problem with it. The church was not selling alcohol. An ABC store shut down, and the church bought the property. There is an old joke in Baptist circles that says, "Jews don't recognize Jesus as the Messiah; Protestants don't recognize the pope as the leader of the Christian faith, and Baptists don't recognize each other at the liquor store." Now, the Baptists that go to that former ABC store, turned church, don't have to wear a disguise.

A newer Christian offense has come out of yoga. There are some well-meaning Christians who have shared how Christians should not do yoga because it has pagan roots. There is this fear that yoga will be a gateway stretch to Satanism. Um...maybe. I mean if doing yoga leads you to worship the Devil or pray pagan prayers then you should avoid it. I'd like to offer another option. Why don't we redeem it? Let me just tell you that I'm not very flexible. Yoga hurts so good. When I'm stretching, the last thing I'm thinking about is joining Satan's army. I'm crying out to God to help me finish this class, and to help me not accidentally fart while doing the downward dog. I don't take yoga classes, but if I did, that's how I imagine they would go. Farting in front of others would be traumatic for me. There is no redemption to be found after letting a fart go accidentally in front of people doing yoga. My point is, if you can use the time to pray, then I don't think you have to worry about what the original intentions of yoga might have been. Redeem it. Take what was created for evil and turn it to God. Greater is the God living in a Christian than the Devil that lives in the world. Live like it.

As a Christian, everything you do represents Jesus. You represent Jesus at your job, with your family, with your friends, and you represent Jesus when you get offended. So, let me ask,

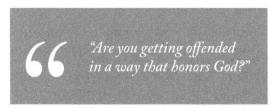

"Are you getting offended in a way that honors God?" The Apostle Paul reminds us that we aren't that different than the culture. He writes...

> At one time we too were foolish, disobedient, deceived and enslaved by all kinds of passions and pleasures. We lived in malice and envy, being hated and hating one another (Titus 3:3).

Paul paints a picture of what it was like before Jesus. In just a minute, we are going to read what it looks like after we believe in Jesus. Paul paints this picture that before Jesus we were foolish. It's been famously said that "The definition of insanity is doing the same thing over and over and expecting different results". If our culture offers offense, then as Christians we have to offer something that tastes better. It is foolish to do the same thing and expect different results. Malice, envy, and hating one another have no place in a Christian's life. Now, we are all human. There are times that we forget who we represent. When we forget, we need to repent and change. Look at what Paul says we are to strive to be:

But when the kindness and love of God our Savior appeared, he saved us, not because of righteous things we had done, but because of his mercy. He saved us through the washing of rebirth and renewal by the Holy Spirit, whom he poured out on us generously through Jesus Christ our Savior, so that, having been justified by his grace, we might become heirs having the hope of eternal life (Titus 3:4-7).

That's Paul's challenge to us. Focus on Jesus. Allow Jesus to change you from the inside out. Focus on the love of Jesus. Accept the kindness of Jesus. By focusing on Jesus, we will be changed. It's like the great theologian Lauren Hill sang, "How you gonna win when you ain't right within?"[9]

I believe that ultimately the reason we get offended is because of something broken inside of us. Ultimately, our offense comes from our own brokenness. We should be so healthy and whole that the actions of others don't control us.

Being offended doesn't make us any different than anyone else. Being offended doesn't change the world. God can change the world, and He wants to start with you. God wants to change us through His kindness. Yelling about how bad things are doesn't change the world. All it does is consume us and push others away. Demanding others change without being willing to change is entitlement. Being offended and complaining isn't doing anyone any good. Remember, the person who offended you is also made in the image of God. God loves and died for

---

9 Lauryn Hill. "Do Wop (That Thing)" The Miseducation of Lauryn Hill. Ruffhouse Records LP, 1988.

the person who offended you. That doesn't mean that we don't speak up. It does mean that we treat others like a fellow child of God. I love the following quote, "The world is changed by your example, not by your opinion."–Paulo Coelho. Don't rush past that too quickly.

WRAPPING THIS UP LIKE A CHRISTMAS PRESENT

If something started out as evil, let's redeem it for the name of Jesus! The Devil has been stealing things from God since the beginning. Let's not just let him take it. Our God is big, and it's time Christians start living in His power — instead of cowering in fear.

Whenever you see something offensive, pray about how God might use you to redeem it for Him. We can do that by remembering that people matter more than offense. There are certain issues we have to stand up for, but in order to win other people over we have to remember that those who don't stand with us are not our enemies. I believe it's natural for humans to cancel things with which we don't agree. It makes sense to me why Christians have lived like

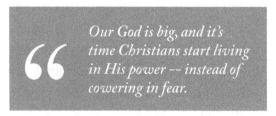

Our God is big, and it's time Christians start living in His power -- instead of cowering in fear.

this for so long. I am urging us to try a better way. We are losing the cultural battle. People care less and less about what we think, and yelling at them is only making it worse. This is why Christians are called to redeem culture and not condemn it.

Questions:

1. Did you grow up celebrating Halloween?

2. Have you ever thought about redeeming culture? If not, what are your thoughts now that you've read this chapter?

3. What are some other examples of redeeming culture? Think of music, movies, restaurants or businesses.

4. What is something that needs to be redeemed in your life?

CHAPTER 10

BE KNOWN FOR WHAT YOU ARE FOR

"If the world hates you because of Jesus, that's expected. If the world hates Jesus because of you, that's a problem."–Dave Adamson.

When you think about Christians, what are some of the thoughts that first come to your mind? For many, it's things like, judgmental, hypocritical, homophobic, and rigid. If those are some of your thoughts then you are not alone.

In a survey, Americans were asked what Christians are known for. The number one answer was "anti-homosexual." Ninety-one percent of unchurched people say the number one thing the modern church is known for is being anti-homosexual.

I believe Christians should hold to the truth of the Scripture, and at the same time we should elevate the good that we do. The truth is that Christians do a lot of amazing things in the world, and have done amazing things for thousands of years. Yet, the number one thing Christians in America are known for is something they are perceived to be against instead of what they are for. The sad truth is that so often the Christians who are doing positive work in the world are too busy doing good to share about it online. As a Christian, I urge other Christians to be so productively living for Jesus that we don't have time to complain about other people. There is a hurting world and a lot of work to do. Unfortunately, in America Christians have lost a lot of influence.

Influence is something that is gained incrementally but lost instantly. We lose influence when we criticize and condemn because when we condemn others, we make them the enemy. When someone feels like they are the enemy, they aren't likely to care about your opinion. Now, if that makes you feel uneasy because you feel we are called to call out the sins of others, please keep reading. I'm not advocating for Christians to not talk about sin. I'm trying to influence to evaluate how we do that. Christians have lost influence in America, so much so, that the good we are doing is being ignored. According to the Barna Research Group, "49% of unchurched Americans cannot identify a single way Christianity has positively impacted the United States."

That's heartbreaking. A Christian invented Chick-fil-A. Christian chicken should count for something. Maybe the 49% don't like pickles on their chicken sandwiches? Christians also started the YMCA, Red Cross, Salvation Army, Hobby Lobby, In-N-Out Burger, and Cook Out. A Christian wrote *Lord of the Rings* and another Christian wrote *The Chronicles of Narnia*. The vast majority of soup kitchens, homeless shelters, and organizations that help the homeless are birthed out of Christians trying to change the world. Almost every pregnancy center, as well as the numerous child sponsorship programs were started by Christians. Barna Research released a study showing that in 2022 Christian philanthropy accounted for 70 percent of all American philanthropy. Christians raised and gave away $300 billion. Barna also pointed out that Christians out-gave the U.S. Government in addressing global poverty. One pastor observed, "Whatever folks might say or think, the church remains a seismic value-add to the world." – Scott Sauls.

Christians have done a lot of good, but it doesn't seem like it's noticed in our culture today. In fact, there is a whole movement to try to cancel Christianity. I've seen it often, especially online. In fact, #cancelchristianity was trending on Twitter during the writing of this book.

This isn't the first time someone has tried to cancel Christianity. In the early days of the Christian faith, Christians were persecuted by the Roman government. Eventually, a great plague and famine swept through Rome, and it caused a lot of people to flee Rome. It's been said that during that time, Christians took better care of the Romans than the Romans did. The way Christians won over the world was by being known for what they were for, not what they were against. One of Jesus' best friends was Peter. He became a leader in the early church and offers these challenging words to the Christians going through persecution.

> Live such good lives among the pagans that, though they accuse you of doing wrong, they may see your good deeds and glorify God on the day he visits us (1 Peter 2:12).

Christians will never be able to fully avoid criticism, and even forms of hatred. The earliest Christians were being killed for their faith, and Peter challenges them to live such a good life that the very people who persecute you can see your good deeds. Way too often, we lead with what we are against. Instead, we should lead with what we are for.

TOLERATE NOT TOLERHATE

Today there doesn't seem to be a lot of room for disagreement – especially, online. The following is how social media seems to work.

Me: I like bananas more than oranges.

Random Person: So, what you are saying is you hate oranges! You failed to mention apples, grapes, and watermelon. Educate yourself! I'm literally shaking at how fruit phobic you are! This is why I don't go to church! I thought pastors weren't supposed to be judgmental!

If you've spent time online, you can relate to that. If that is what it feels like to be online, then Christians have an amazing opportunity to provide something radically different. The Apostle Paul tells us how to do that in the following verses:

As a prisoner for the Lord, then, I urge you to live a life worthy of the calling you have received. Be completely humble and gentle; be patient, *bearing with one another in love.* Make every effort to keep the unity of the Spirit through the bond of peace (Ephesians 4:1-3 — Italics mine).

There is a lot to unpack in these verses, but did you notice that it did not say anything about boycotting, avoiding, or going to war? Paul understood that in every relationship there will be some drama. There will be offense. He challenges Christians, especially with each other, to bear with one another. Now, to bear with one another does not mean to act like a mama bear after her cubs have been stolen and starts swinging at anyone who offends you. Instead, the word here means to hold up or tolerate. I love what Pastor Larry Osborne says about tolerance and Christians.

> "Tolerance is a trait we should excel in. If tolerance means granting people the right to be wrong, we of all people ought to be known for our tolerance." – Larry Osborne

I don't see a lot of tolerance today. I see a lot of tribalism that aims to destroy anyone who disagrees with it. The fear is that we cannot tolerate anyone who is wrong. The truth is, you can bear with or tolerate someone while confronting a hurtful behavior. This takes lots of grace, patience, and love.

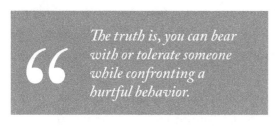

The truth is, you can bear with or tolerate someone while confronting a hurtful behavior.

When we are in war, the goal is to destroy the other side. Offense is a hurt. If we do not deal with it in a healthy way, we end up looking for ways to punish the other side. We do this through all sorts of ways. We fight; we construct arguments to destroy; we block or hide people, or we gossip behind their backs; we post passive aggressive messages online, etc. What Paul says is radical and in tune with what Jesus wants us to do. Paul's challenge to us is to reach out to the very people who offend us. I love what Pastor Tim Keller says,

"A shortcoming of our current society is we don't
reason with the other side, we only denounce.
Where is the space to do this?"–Tim Keller

Tim Keller asks "Where is the space to do this?" I think
it should be at church and within the Christian community. I
believe Christians should be the safest people around. Truth
is not insecure, so we shouldn't be either. What I mean is that
since what we believe is true, we shouldn't get defensive when
others don't believe it. We don't have to fight for the truth. We
don't have to shove the truth down people's throats. Because
we believe in the truth, we can grant others the right to be
wrong. That's how we tolerate others. We have to extend some
patience, knowing that people can change, and change takes
time. We need to hold firmly to what we believe, but show
grace and patience to those who disagree. Instead of getting
offended, Paul challenges us to pull up a chair, have a conversation and, in humility, bear with one another.

This can't happen if we are committed to being offended.
Listen, if your offense is changing the world, then hold on to it.
If your offense is getting results and helping people love Jesus
more, then I want to learn from you. It's been my experience
that when we humble ourselves, admit that we don't have all
the answers, hold tight to the truth, and show love to those we
disagree with, that we can see progress. What would happen if
we worked on being committed to bear with one another? What
would happen if, before we considered holding a grudge, we
committed to having a conversation? What would happen if we
made a decision to put relationships over our personal offense?
I believe we would change the world.

This is messy! As a pastor I want my church to be a safe place for broken people. We accommodate but, at the same time, have standards. It means we are willing to have difficult conversations. When someone on our volunteer team at church is not honoring God, we have a conversation. Sometimes, that leads to asking people to take a break from serving or to step down from the team. They are more than welcome to still attend the church. Because we do our best to share the standards ahead of time, we have had conversations that went really well. We asked someone to step down, and the person understood where we were coming from. We have also had multiple examples of people who left angry. In every case, I've done my best to try and continue to show them kindness.

In some ways, it's like eating at a restaurant. If I own the restaurant, I get to set the menu. A restaurant will do its best to accommodate my tastes if they fit within their menu. If I go to a burger place and want a plain cheese burger (because mayo is siphoned liposuction from the Hollywood elite, and mustard is gag nasty), most restaurants will accommodate me. However, if I go to a burger restaurant and request a pizza, they will most likely tell me, "That's not on the menu." As a Christian, I aim to be clear about what I believe; that's my burger. We shouldn't expect everyone to like it. I'll do my best to accommodate you, but if you want me to do something that is not on the Christian menu, I won't be able to help you. I can be kind, but I cannot do something others want me to if it goes against Scripture. I think the following quote teaches us how to do that well.

> "The best way to show that a stick is crooked
> is not to argue about it or to spend time

denouncing it, but to lay a straight stick along-side it."–DL Moody.

I agree with that whole heartedly. The best way to fight against a crooked stick is to find a better example. Instead of ranting against culture, let's show culture what we are truly about! We don't have to yell and scream against the darkness! We can be a light by showing a better way. The best way to fight against an ungodly culture is not to yell at it. The best way is to show it a better way to live! We do that when we champion what we are for.

The key is to promote and talk more about what we are for than what we are against. We champion what we are for so much that it's what people think about more than what we are against. We don't think burger restaurants are anti-pizza restaurants because they only serve burgers. In the same way, Christians should be so known for their love because we serve love so well. I don't expect a non-Christian to behave like a Christian. This applies to how we treat other Christians, as well. I often see someone online take a stance against a church because the person doesn't agree with the pastor's theology. In the comments, I can see that their stance has gathered people who already agree with them and divided those who like the pastor. I have yet to see a change of mind happen. What if, instead of making a post against the church you disagree with, you make a post about what you are for? The church has lost its influence in America, but I believe we can get it back. It starts with every Christian doing their part to influence the world.

Questions:

1. What does it mean to be known for what you are for instead of what you are against?

2. Out of the three ways to gain influence, which one do you do the best?

3. Out of the three ways to gain influence, which one do you have the most room for improvement?

4. What is your next step to improve in this area?

CHAPTER 11

THE GOSPEL AND OFFENSE

"I do all this for the sake of the gospel, that I may
share in its blessings"–Paul

I believe the key to influence people is for Christians to be all
about the gospel. This is what we should ultimately be for!
If we are going to offend someone, may it be because of the
gospel. By the way, our goal should not be to offend, but it
will happen.

I believe we should be preaching, talking, and sharing
about the things
we are for. We
should be known
for the gospel!
Remember what

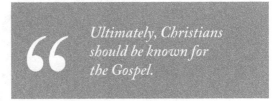

Ultimately, Christians
should be known for
the Gospel.

Paul says about being all about the Gospel?

> I have become all things to all people so that
> by all possible means I might save some. I do
> all this for <u>the sake of the gospel</u>, that I may
> share in its blessings, and belong to no one, I

115

have made myself a slave to everyone, to win as many as possible (1 Corinthians 9:22-23).

Ultimately, Christians should be known for the Gospel. The following is how I believe we can do just that. I believe what you are about to see will help you know when to speak up and when to stay silent. It will also help you become less offended. It's called the Theological Triage. I first learned about this from Theologian Russell Moore. I've adapted it from what he originally did, but I want to give credit where credit is due.

THEOLOGICAL TRIAGE

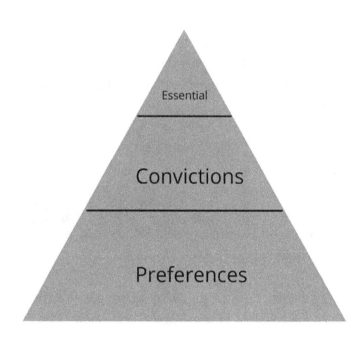

I think it is very helpful in helping us learn to be unified. It's incredibly important for us in order to learn how to be known for what we are for instead of what we are against. Triage is a French word that means to sort. In the emergency room, professionals are trained to sort patients based on their greatest risk. So, someone who comes in with a heart attack is going to have priority over someone who comes in with a splinter. This idea can help Christians understand what is a disputable matter and what is not. The triage is made up of three sections.

Triage

1. Essential

2. Convictions

3. Preferences

THE ESSENTIAL

This first one is where I've adapted the triage from others that I've seen. There are lots of debatable things within Christianity. These things are important and can help us understand God, but they are not essential to salvation. The Gospel is the essential in Christianity. Without it, a person is not a Christian. So, what is the Gospel? That's a great question. Thanks for asking it.

The Gospel is the belief that humans are born sinful, but saved by grace by Jesus' death, burial, and resurrection. It's the understanding that through Jesus' sacrifice we have new life. We cannot earn this grace of Jesus because it's a gift that He willingly gave.

The Gospel is essential because it will help you know how to engage with people. Did you know that Christians are called to deal with Christians and non-Christians differently? Look at what the Apostle Paul writes,

> What business is it of mine to judge those outside the church? Are you not to judge those inside? God will judge those outside. "Expel the wicked person from among you" (1 Corinthians 5:12-13).

Those are some pretty harsh words, and there is some explaining to be done. Paul is addressing the sexual immorality that was going on in the church of Corinth. Paul's ultimate goal was to win back the sexually immoral Christian. Paul calls for church discipline to correct the bad behavior. And, it worked! We read in 2 Corinthians that the sexually immoral person is back at the church and Paul encourages the church to show him grace and forgiveness. Paul's overall point though is that Christians are called to hold each other accountable with truth and grace. At the same time, Paul challenges us not to judge those who are not Christians. Non-Christians aren't held to the same standards of Christians because they don't know Jesus.

If you are bucking against Paul's words, let me encourage you to reframe your thinking. Discipline is a necessary part of excellence. We don't want to be shamed, yelled at, or manipulated, but there are healthy forms of discipline. Think about a good coach for sports. Great coaches do a lot more than simply call plays and make substitutions. They have to coach the players by calling them to a higher standard. That includes dealing with bad attitudes, laziness, and other negative behaviors.

I often think about a scene in one of my favorite movies, *The Karate Kid*. In the movie, Daniel has promised to learn karate from his karate teacher, Mr. Miyagi. So far, Daniel hasn't done a lot of karate training. If you saw the movie, you remember "Wax on, wax off." Daniel signed up to learn karate, but instead he has learned to wash and wax cars, paint the fence, and sand the deck. Daniel has had enough, and in anger, he explodes on Mr. Miyagi. He uses way too many curse words for a movie that is rated PG, but it was the 80s and PG-13 wasn't invented yet. Mr. Miyagi doesn't get offended. He simply takes control of the situation and coaches Daniel. He uses all the authority he has and tells Daniel to show him "Wax on, wax off." Daniel does the motion with a lot of attitude and some mocking. And then, my favorite scene appears. Mr. Miyagi says, "Att tat tat tat." If you haven't seen it, you should watch it just for this scene. With this little phrase, Mr. Miyagi corrects Daniel's bad attitude and redirects him to do the motion correctly. It's a brilliant coaching move! This scene is what I think about when I consider church discipline. Church discipline's goal is to coach and ultimately cause the other person to return. I believe we don't have stronger Christians because most Christians don't have a coach who believes in them enough to call out their potential by coaching or correcting them.

When dealing with people, the Gospel is the essential because it helps us know if we are dealing with another Christian or not. Christians are in the wrong when they judge the world by Christian standards. Christians should pray for the lost, look for opportunities to influence the world, and be careful not to be influenced negatively. So, when dealing with culture, Christians should lose the outrage when the world acts—worldly. Christians should stop being surprised when people sin, vote differently, or do things that do not align with Scripture. The essential for Christians is the Gospel. That leads us to the second part of the triage.

CONVICTIONS

The second part of the triage is convictions. This is often where Christians fight. Convictions are important for you in selecting a church. For example, I am friends with people who believe very different things than I do about baptism. They believe in infant baptism. My church doesn't practice infant baptism. I respect their opinion and have listened with an open ear, but I disagree. We can still be friends, but this is such a big topic that we would have a difficult time leading a church together.

Gender roles in church is another very divisive issue. In some circles, a woman preaching is celebrated and normal. In others, it is right up there with any sinful abomination. Debatable topics like whether a Christian should consume alcohol, practice spiritual gifts like speaking in tongues, and other matters where each side uses Scripture to support the viewpoint are convictions. Convictions are important! In fact, I wish more Christians knew what their convictions were before they join a church. Way too often, I see individuals visit a church and fall in love with the preaching or kids programming only to find out two years later their convictions do not line up with the church. At that point if the person leaves the church, it is often ugly. Feelings get hurt. When someone has a conviction, it is very personal. When someone else disagrees, it feels like an attack. Way too many people are deconstructing their faith and it's because they were offended or didn't get their way.

When I meet someone who is upset about one of these issues, I try to say in love, "Next Level may not be the right church for you, and that's okay. We still love you, but that's not who we are." Convictions are important, but they are not the Gospel.

Convictions can vary from Christian or church. I know people who join a seeker sensitive church and love it for two to three years. Once the honeymoon phase ends, they start to complain about the church. What they want are deeper sermons and more traditional church songs. They often forget that they left the traditional church for a reason. A frustration is never content until it's expressed so they complain to anyone who will listen. The problem is the church didn't change. The church didn't pull a bait and switch on them. The church is fulfilling its stated mission.

The issue is a person who holds a different value or conviction, but has not discovered it until two years into the relationship. In order to be less triggered, you and I need to accept that not every Christian will share our convictions, and that's okay. It might mean we cannot go to church together. It might mean we have to establish some safe boundaries. It should mean that we can be friends and disagree. That takes us to the third part of the triage.

PREFERENCES

The third part of the triage is preferences. Preferences are things that are important to us, but not Scriptural. Some preferences I have seen are style of music in church. Singing hymns vs. singing praise songs can be a preference. Dressing up in church vs. casual dress can be a preference. Here's one that may ruffle some feathers; the Bible translation that you use is a preference. The Bible never tells us to only use King James because the King James Bible wasn't around when the Bible was being written. Anything in your life that is important to you, but not based on a Scriptural conviction is a preference. It's okay to have preferences, but we often turn our preferences into convictions or into an essential. This is where we cause major damage. We condemn someone because it's different, and not necessarily because it's wrong.

I was once told I was going to Hell because I don't use the King James Bible. King James wasn't perfect, and he is not my God. He did not die for my sins. I may or may not have told this person a historical fact about King James. I'm not proud of it. I'm a work in progress. It was in my younger days, and I may have been triggered. I quickly pointed out that King James had homosexual tendencies. His translation is

> *Feel free to go to a church that keeps kids in the service, but be careful not to condemn other churches that have different preferences.*

FABULOUS, but it's not an essential to salvation. That shut the person down quickly, but wasn't a good move on my part. Remember, I'm a work in progress.

Another preference that I see divides the church over kids' ministry. I know some Christians are very passionate that kids should be in big church with their families. This is often based on how they were raised. It is important to them, but it should not be fought over in churches. The Scriptures are silent about whether kids should sit in big church or go to an age-appropriate environment to learn about Jesus. Feel free to go to a church that keeps kids in the service, but be careful not to condemn other churches that have different preferences.

Here's another example that I see Christians fight about—exegetical preaching or topical preaching. I've heard entire sermons on why exegetical preaching is the only option. Exegetical preaching is where a pastor preaches line by line and book by book through the Bible. For example, I was once at a church where the pastor preached through John for three years. The problem with saying this is the only way to preach is the Bible does not tell us that. It may indeed be the best way to preach, but that would be a preference, and in my opinion, not a conviction. Preferences matter, but they should not cause divisions between believers.

DISPUTABLE MATTERS

The Apostle Paul says, "Accept the one whose faith is weak, without quarreling over disputable matters" (Romans 14:1).

Accept one whose faith is weak? What Paul is talking about here is a serious issue in the church. He is going to talk more about this later in the chapter, but what you need to know is that the things people were fighting about were very important to them.

That leads to a question. Why are our beliefs so important to us?

The church Paul was writing to was fighting about religious holidays and eating certain foods. Today we don't fight about the same issues they fought about, but the heart is the same. Our beliefs and opinions are very important to us. Have you ever asked the question why?

Humans are tribal creatures. According to psychology, we often find our identity in things we have in common with others. In order for that to happen, we have to identify others who are different. So, by nature, we are wired to unite with those with whom we agree, and vilify those with whom we disagree.

Think about this for just a moment. One of the most basic human desires is to have in groups and out groups. This is not based on policies or convictions. It's based on the desire to fit in with people who support you. In order to fit in, there has to be a group that doesn't fit in. That group is the out group, and our brains naturally look at them as the enemy. This is why we so often fight passionately about preferences. We want people to agree with us and when they don't, we struggle. In fact, when someone disagrees with us, our brains look for reasons why. We think, "Surely, the other person disagrees because they are fundamentally flawed."

Don't miss this. We do this naturally as humans. Below are some common preferences that divide us. I want you to look at them and take a side.

Coke vs. Pepsi.
Mayo vs. Miracle Whip.
Michael Jordan vs. Lebron James.
Apple vs. Android.

Okay, did you pick a side? Maybe you don't care about each one of these examples, but pick one that you care the most about. Now, think about how you feel about people who disagree with you on this topic. Typically, people who chose one, do not love the fact that someone would choose something else. With these examples, we don't see a lot of fist fights. However, if you listen, you can hear a lot of insults.

I know people who so prefer Coke that they will not visit a restaurant that serves Pepsi. When I've told people that I don't discriminate against full calorie sodas, they push back and tell me I have to choose. I cannot tell you how many times someone has looked at me like I have a nipple on my face when I say I like Coke and Pepsi. Some will declare, "You CAN'T!"

I can, and I do. Don't move past this too quickly. What I am getting at is that it is human nature to find people with whom we agree, and to push back against people with whom we disagree. Once we have chosen a side we then look to criticize the other side. This is problematic. It causes us to dismiss those we disagree with. Christian musician Ross King has some insight on this that is full of truth.

> "A right action done by a person we don't like
> is still right. A wrong action done by someone
> we like is still wrong. This is hard because we
> don't like to give any ground to 'the other side,'
> either in admitting one of 'them' did something
> right or one of 'us' did something wrong."

We see this type of thinking a lot in politics; the other side is full of evil people who don't know what they are doing and if they are in power Democracy will end.

There was a social psychology experiment in the 1950s that illustrates this perfectly. The social experiment was called "Robbers Cave." In the experiment, a group of fifth-grade boys—all white, middle-class and Protestant were divided into two groups at a summer camp in Oklahoma. Notice that the two groups had everything in common. They came from the same type of families, same gender, race, and age. The only real difference was that the camp divided the boys into two separate groups. Within two weeks, the two groups devolved into insulting and threatening each other. It got so bad that those who were running the experiment had to intervene. The simple difference of being placed in a different group caused so much conflict they had to stop the experiment.

"Us" vs. "Them" thinking is destructive and has no place in the Christian life. It is natural to pick sides, but Jesus calls us to reach across the aisle and love the side we disagree with. There are so many things that divide us, but one major thing that should unite Christians. We should be united over the Gospel! Did you know that unity in the church is more important than agreement on debatable, less significant matters in the Christian life. Disputable matters should not disrupt Christian oneness. Look once again at what Paul wrote,

> "Accept the one whose faith is weak, without quarreling over disputable matters" (Romans 14:1, my own underline).

Now, the question that we have to ask is what is a disputable matter? Our identity has become so tangled with our politics that everything seems important. Our opinions are so often attached to our identity that everything that does not align with what we believe feels like an issue worthy of quarreling. How do we know what we should dispute and what we should let go? This is where the Theological Triage helps.

If someone has a belief that is different than yours, the first thing that is important to find out is if the person is a Christian or not. If a person is not a Christian, then your approach should be to influence, pray, and attempt to win them over. It's not worth arguing or debating because your foundation is different. If the person who has a different belief than yours is a Christian then you move to the next level of the triage. Is this issue a conviction? If it is then be careful trying to change the person. This is where you may have to agree to disagree. This is where you find unity around the Gospel, and do your best to respect the differences. You may not be in a position to go to church together, and you may not want to do a Bible study with the person, but you can still be friends. Do not attack, and I would not recommend debating or arguing if it's going to ruin the friendship. In fact, Paul would say to respect the person and do your best to honor the person's conviction. In other words, don't rub it in their face that you have a different conviction.

If you are ever in a place where you are looking for a church, make sure that you share some convictions or at least find out what the church's convictions are. If an issue between Christians is a preference, then 100% you should not quarrel over it. When a preference gets elevated to an essential item, you have an idol. Any preference that becomes an idol will get in the way of your relationship with Jesus and His people. If someone has a preference that is an idol, they may have to be corrected. They should be corrected in truth and love. The goal though is to maintain unity.

Now, both convictions and preferences can be disputable matters. Every conviction that is birthed out of Scripture has someone else who has a different conviction also birthed out of Scripture. Paul says don't quarrel over these. Have your opinions, have your convictions, but stop tearing each other down because of these differences.

This applies to politics! You ever notice how with every political issue there is a dispute? Paul would not say to abandon your convictions! This is important! You can have your convictions.

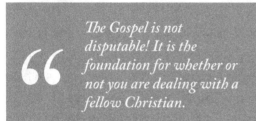

The Gospel is not disputable! It is the foundation for whether or not you are dealing with a fellow Christian.

In fact, Paul says to stick with your convictions. However, don't fight with other people over disputable matters. The Gospel is not disputable! It is the foundation for whether or not you are dealing with a fellow Christian. Everything else is something that has been disputed for thousands of years.

Paul goes on to describe the issues over which the church in Rome is fighting. They are dietary issues and obeying the Sabbath. Let's look at what Paul says,

> You, then, why do you judge your brother or sister? Or why do you treat them with contempt? For we will all stand before God's judgment seat. It is written: "'As surely as I live,' says the Lord, 'every knee will bow before me; every tongue will acknowledge God.'" So then, each of us will give an account of ourselves to God (Romans 14:10-12).

This is so important! If you are a Christian, you are forgiven from all of your sins. You cannot lose God's love. At the same time, when we die, we will give an account for ourselves and a part of that account is how we loved people. The Scriptures say we will give an account for every careless word. That's why I don't say things like decaf coffee. It's pointless. I'm kidding. So, because we will give an account, Paul then says,

> "Therefore, let us stop passing judgment on one another. Instead, make up your mind not to put any stumbling block or obstacle in the way of a brother or sister" (Romans 14:13).

Did you catch what Paul said? Stop passing judgment on one another, and at the same time make up your mind not to put a stumbling block in the way of another Christian. If your conviction is that Christians can drink alcohol, don't judge other Christians who have a different conviction, and at the same time don't flaunt your alcohol in front of them. In other words, "Do not quarrel over disputable matters!"

The triage is not meant to show you when to get offended. It is more of a guide to use to help you know how to respond in your offense. When it is time to engage with someone who offends you, it's important that you do so in a way that still represents Christ. If it's a gospel issue then we need to ask if the other person is a believer or not. If they are a believer and it's a gospel issue then we can confront in love. The goal should be to coach and not to destroy the other person. If it's not a gospel issue and they are a believer we need to ask if it's a conviction. Convictions are important, but they shouldn't lead to fighting We should know our convictions and be secure enough in them that we allow others to be wrong. We don't flaunt our freedom in front of others and we also shouldn't judge others who have a different conviction. If it's a conviction it should come from

Scripture! If it's not a conviction then it's a preference. This is where we have to show lots of grace. If it's a preference I don't have to try and convince someone else they are wrong. I also don't have to send an email to the pastor to try and convince him to change something.

The theological triage helps us gain influence by knowing how to respond to each person. We often treat each offense the same. The first thing we need to do is stop holding non Christians to Christian standards. When it comes to Christians we can lose influence when we overact to an offense. Knowing the triage will help us stay on target and ensure we are staying focused on the gospel. There is almost nothing more attractive than Christians living in unity, and almost nothing more repelling than Christians fighting with one another.

Questions:

1. Why is understanding the Theological Triage helpful for dealing with offense?

2. Have you ever thought about responding differently to non-Christians than you do to Christians?

3. Based on your understanding, explain the theological triage to someone who hasn't read this book.

4. What are some examples of preferences in your life? What are some examples of convictions?

PART III

O ne of the challenges of having influence comes from the fact that we have to be in somewhat close proximity in order to have influence. It is difficult to influence people you don't know or who don't know you. In Part Three, I want to share one of the greatest ways we can build influence. You may never become a YouTube celebrity or an Instagram influencer, but you can be a great friend. My hope through this section is that, by becoming a better friend, you will get offended less, and at the same time, do something productive with your offense.

I want to give a little more explanation before we get to the next chapter because I can see why this would seem like a hard right turn for some. What does friendship have to do with getting offended? As I mentioned above, it is an amazing way to gain influence. It's also, in my opinion, the most practical way to change someone's mind. Arguing online doesn't change anyone's mind. Fighting about the latest outrage from our culture doesn't change very many opinions. On the other hand, I have seen people changed through relationships. I've seen people of different races form strong friendships, Republicans and Democrats form strong friendships, and even Baptists and Charismatics form strong friendships. That's a minor miracle! If you want to change, focus on your friendships. People are changed way more by relationships than opinions.

The entire Bible can be summed up by learning how to love God and love others. When it comes to making decisions, Christians should have these two filters in place. Does this help me love God more, and does this help me love others?

Way too often, people put offense over the relationship. I believe we should strive to put the relationship ahead of the offense. As a pastor, I constantly feel like relationships are based off a bartering system instead of deep care. I absolutely love my job and enjoy being a pastor! At the same time, I've seen way too many people leave a church because of offense. People seem to love each other when they get their way and agree, but as soon as there is a disagreement, the relationship is discarded. I've seen people I deeply care for leave the church without even having a conversation. I get it, relationships are messy. Being a part of a church is messy. So is being a part of a family. Every relationship will have some degree of offense.

When offense is put first, friendships end, families break up, churches split, and relationships are impacted. Here's the deal; everyone you know will offend you at some point. When you put people first, you will learn to deal with the offense in a healthy way.

When we put relationships first, we will be willing to have the difficult conversation. Putting the relationship first doesn't mean you ignore tough things. It means you work hard at solving issues together. Because we believe the relationship is worth fighting for, we should have respectful, but tough, conversations whenever offense happens.

When you hold on to anger, bury frustration, or refuse to talk, it's ultimately revealing that you don't feel like the relationship is worth fighting for. When you fight first because of an offense, you are showing that your opinion is more important than the relationship. The key to dealing with offense in a healthy manner is to lead with friendship. When you feel the need to confront, remember to start with the friendship. It is crucial to remember friendship and to give that more weight than the offense. When we put offense first, we forget that there is another person on the other side of that offense. In healthy relationships, it is important to start with friendship, confront, and then end with friendship in mind.

In order for friendship to be an effective filter for how we respond to people, we need to define friend. For a lot of people, friendship is a broad term. In this section, I want to define a true friend. By doing that, we will learn how to process our offense with various people.

CHAPTER 12

WE CAN DISAGREE AND STILL BE FRIENDS

"You can maybe change laws with violent protests, but you can't change hearts."– Philip Yancey

As a pastor, I unintentionally offend people on a regular basis. There are a lot of Karens out there. Okay, if your name is Karen, I want to say that I'm sorry for what the Internet has done with your name. At some point, the Internet said "Goodbye" to Felicia and "Hello" to Karen. I love multiple people with the name Karen. If you don't have a fat clue what I'm talking about, ask someone under the age of 35. Just in case you are too lazy to do that, I'll explain it quickly. The Internet has dubbed "Karen" as someone who is entitled and who complains. It's typically a white woman and, for some reason, they all have the same haircut.

There are a lot of Karens out there, and it makes dealing with offense tricky. It's easy to label everyone who complains a Karen. I'm not sure that is helpful. Not all complaints are from Karens. At the same time, when you have a complaint, it is important to make sure that you deliver it in a way that is helpful. I often get messages like the one below. If you have a pastor, please know he gets messages like this regularly, as well. It's important for you to read, in order to learn what not to do with your offense.

Dear Pastor Rob,

I just wanted to reach out and give you my thoughts on Sunday's sermon. I was disappointed with the content and the lack of Scripture. I felt like it was an infomercial.

I was excited to come to church on Sunday, but when I saw that it was a Q & A, I quickly tuned it out. My husband missed church on Sunday because he was golfing. I had him listen to the podcast so that he would understand where I was coming from. He agrees with me 100%. In fact, there are a lot of people who feel the same way as I do. Everyone is talking about it. Is that the kind message you want to portray?

Now, maybe it's because I'm not a fan of Q & A services or maybe it's because I don't think there is enough Scripture given. I am not sure, but it was heavy on my mind, so I wanted to bring it up to you and ask you what you thought about Sunday's sermon? Is this going to be a regular occurrence? If so, can you let me know so I can stay home on those Sundays?

You always say to talk to the person and not about the person, so that is what I am doing. I look forward to your response.

Best regards,

Karen

Complaints stink! Criticism really stinks. They are going to come. You cannot avoid them. That fictitious message fails miserably because it doesn't take the other person into account. It only focuses on the writer's perspective and fails to find any connection. Letters like that can make the author feel better, but they don't change the other person. In fact, they will often fall on deaf ears or cause a rift in the relationship. I believe letters like the one above are not helpful for putting the relationship first. They are helpful in helping the offended person feel better, but when you ask, "What good did my offense (letter) do," I believe you will see that it did little good for the relationship. President Abraham Lincoln is famous for writing a "Hot Letter." It's a letter full of candor, where he vented, and got all of his frustration out. He would wait until he cooled down, revisit the letter and then write, "Never sent, never signed." This is such a practical tool. Today we could apply this to emails or social media comments. When we are offended, we tend to react and very rarely does that reaction help strengthen the relationship.

When we get offended, we tend to put the offense first. What matters most is that we are hurt and want to do something about it. Friendship is important because it can help us to put the relationship first. When someone is a true friend, we should put the relationship ahead of the offense. Many relationships don't make it because offense separates people. I believe with all my heart that we can disagree and still be friends. It may mean that we write some letters and never send them. It might mean that we have to vent to God, but no other person will ever hear about our anger. It may mean that we have to wait until we cool down to have a hard conversation. I believe President Lincoln demonstrated how we can disagree and still be friends. That phrase has become very important to me. You will disagree, but I want you to do it in a way that puts the relationship first.

YOU CAN'T BE SERIOUS

I believe with all my heart that we can disagree and still be friends. It's not easy, but from my experience, it's a lot less exhausting then being offended all of the time.

Disagreement always leads to a divide. In order to bridge the gap, someone has to decide to put the friendship first. Have you ever been in an argument that went nowhere? Someone rants and then a different person rants about their rant. Before you know it, an argument breaks out. If you are not intentional, that disagreement will get personal, really quickly. Name calling and insults are the norm when a disagreement happens. It's kind of like this fake Facebook post...

That escalated quickly! The Internet has been hating on the band Nickelback for years. Nobody knows why. I used them because it's a silly example, but don't miss the truth to it. So often online disagreements will lead to a division. This happens because people put offense over relationships.

THINK

So, what do you do if you have a strong opinion and you want to share it? I love the following acronym that was created to help bring more peaceful online interactions. The THINK acronym is helpful for sharing online. It was created to help stop bullying and negativity.

T–Is it true? Have you fact checked it?
H–Is it helpful?
I–Is it inspiring?
N–Is it necessary?
K–Is it kind?

Not every thought you have is worth sharing. Not every opinion that you have needs to be shared. One time, someone left the church I pastor, but remained friends with me on social media. Over the next year, when I would share something about church on Facebook, this person would say, "I no longer go to Next Level but..." Um...thanks Karen (not this person's real name), but that is not helpful. This person passed the first test. It was true that the person was no longer going to the church I pastor. It was not helpful, inspiring, or necessary. Please know, not every post online is for you. Not every post on Facebook needs your opinion. Please don't be the person who doesn't add value to the conversation! Have you ever posted something like, "Looking for restaurant recommendations," and someone will post, "I don't eat out." That's not helpful! Strive to be a person that adds value and not just opinions. Add value to your conversations, meetings, social media interactions.

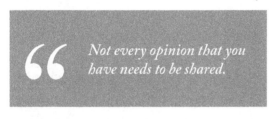

Not every opinion that you have needs to be shared.

Now, you might feel some pressure from this. If you are thinking, "Well, then, I just won't share any opinions ever!" Hold the phone on that response. There is a place for disagreement. There is a place for another opinion. The place to share opinions is with friends. If you are not in a relationship with someone, then pull an Elsa from *Frozen*, and "Let it go." You won't change them anyway. If, however, you are friends with someone, then you have the relational equity to have tough conversations.

HOW TO DISAGREE AND STILL BE FRIENDS

I want to finish what I promised at the beginning of this chapter, and that is show how to disagree and still be friends. The key to disagreeing and still being a friend is to put the friendship first. When we put offense first, we fight unfair, name call, avoid, block, and unfriend. When we put friendship first, we will have a tough conversation, but we will do it in a way that seeks resolution.

Remember the letter near the beginning of this chapter? When I get letters like that, it rarely changes my opinion. In your anger you may need to write a letter like that, but please don't send it. Instead, wait until you calm down, and send a letter that puts the friendship first. Contrast the first letter with the following letter.

Dear Pastor Rob,

I just wanted to reach out and give you my thoughts on Sunday's sermon. I love our church, and I care about you. I know you juggle a lot. Please know that what I'm about to write does not change how I feel about you or our church.

Because I care about you, I wanted to bring my concern to you. I haven't talked to anyone else about this. I know doing Q & A services are difficult. I can't imagine giving answers right on the spot. With that being said, is there a way to include more Scripture in the Q & A? I don't want to bring problems without solutions so here is my idea. Feel free to dismiss it. What if, on the Q & A week, we have someone from the church or staff read a Scripture? This might be too old school of an idea, but we could even do a responsive reading. That way Scripture is still highlighted.

I support you and always look forward to the Q & A. If you don't agree, please know I still support you. You do such an amazing job of highlighting and explaining Scripture, and I miss that on weeks when we do a Q & A. I look forward to hearing your thoughts.

Better together,

Karen

Do you see the difference? Negativity weighs more than positivity, so you have to be intentional and make sure that the other person knows you care about and support him or her. If you don't make that clear, you run the risk of your negative words doing more damage than good. We can disagree and still be friends, but that doesn't mean that you unload on someone when you disagree with him or her. The first letter led with the offense, but the second letter led with friendship. It's not enough to tell someone how you feel. If you want real change, you must consider the other person, and friendship helps us do that.

In order to disagree and still be friends, we have to intentionally hold onto the friendship. The next time you are in a disagreement, try saying the following, "I may disagree with you on this, but it won't change how I feel about you. You will always be my friend (or I will always love you if it applies). When we argue with others, one of the fears that immediately creeps in is, does this mean the other person is going to leave? It's one reason so many of us hate conflict. We have a fear that people will leave if conflict happens. To

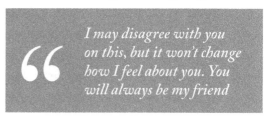

I may disagree with you on this, but it won't change how I feel about you. You will always be my friend

help with that, let the other person know how you feel. Put the friendship, first. Lead with the friendship, first. Show the other person that you aren't going anywhere. If you can't lead with the friendship first, then you need to take some time to cool off until you can. This leads to the next chapter of this section, "What is a friend?" In order to put friendship above offense, we need to define what a true friend is. I'll see you in the next chapter.

Questions:

1. Can you recall a time you were offended and responded in that offense? What did you do?

2. Looking back over how you handled that offense, what would you do differently now?

3. Is it easy or more difficult for you to believe the best when someone offends you?

4. How can leading with friendship save you from some unnecessary drama?

5. What are some things you can do to help your-self remember to ask clarifying questions when you are offended?

CHAPTER 13

WHAT IS A FRIEND?

"I would rather walk with a friend in the dark,
than alone in the light." -Helen Keller

In order to put friendship ahead of offense, we need to have good friends and be a good friend. In this chapter, I aim to define what a friend is. You'll find that once you know what a true friend is, it allows you to manage your expectations better and become offended less. Friendship is incredibly important to humans. We are wired to need other people. Maybe you are familiar with the saying:

"Show me your friends, and I'll show you your future."

That's a powerful quote. It reminds me of the famous friendship quote:

"You're the average of the five people you spend the most time with." Jim Rohn

I believe in both of those quotes. In fact, I've experienced them. I believe we are better together. We are all influencing and being influenced by someone. I think most people would say that friendships are good, but yet according to research, a former Surgeon General has noted that the next great health crisis is going to be the lack of friendships.

We have more ways than ever to be connected with people, and yet, we are the least connected we have ever been. Being connected and having great friendships is so important for both mental and physical health.

People with more social connections are happier and healthier in a host of ways, such as the following :[10]

- lower blood pressure

- lower body mass index (BMI)

- less likely to experience depression

- live up to 22 percent longer

The health benefits show that having friends is good for you. Seriously, it lowers your body mass index! I'm a big guy; I can't imagine how much bigger I would be if I didn't have good friends. I believe everyone can apply what we are going to learn in this section, but I want to take a moment to speak specifically to men. In a recent survey, 2.5 million men admitted to having no close friends.

---

[10] National Library of Medicine. Published 2015, October 7. Authors Jessica Martino, Jennifer Pegg, Elizabeth Pegg Frates https://www.ncbi.nlm.nih.gov/pmc/articles/PMC6125010/

The reason this happens is because when a man starts dating, his attention moves from friends to his girlfriend. If he gets married, his attention is spent on his wife. Then if he has kids, his attention moves to them. Men tend to focus on how to provide for their families and that means they spend a lot of time at the job. Because men tend to spend a lot of time at the job, they want to prioritize family time when they are not at work. Men tend to not be great at multitasking, so friendships are often one of the things that gets left by the wayside. Based on research, most men don't have great friends, and the ramifications of this are tremendous.

Research shows that when men have healthy friendships they process and handle stress better. When a man lacks friends, it is linked to significantly higher rates of depression, anxiety, and death. In fact, one Johns Hopkins study found blood pressure rates improved 17 percent when men suffering from heart disease had the support of friends and a spouse, as opposed to just a spouse. Don't move past that too quickly. The key to that research is having a spouse and friend, not either or. The University of Michigan researched friendship and found that being a part of a social group gives a 67 percent improvement in symptoms of depression.

The health benefits happen when men have both the support of friends and a spouse. This is important because many men don't have great friends. They may have companions. They may also have friends who were from ages ago that they can pick back up with any time they see each other, but in reality they don't often see each other. Comedian John Mulroney addressed this in his standup routine featured on Saturday Night Live. This is funny, but there is some insight to what he says. Mulroney jokes that married men don't have friends.

"They have spouses who have friends that have husbands." It's been my experience that his joke hits close to real life. A lot of men simply don't have great friends.

Whether you are a man or a woman, friendship is incredibly important to your health and happiness. Most churches have some form of small groups. There are multiple clubs and hobbies that aim to help people get connected. Social media has allowed us to be more connected than ever, but yet, the stats of loneliness are increasing. The key is not to simply be surrounded by people. It's to have meaningful relationships. I believe the problem is, we don't have a great definition of what a friend is. When we learn what a true friend is, we should aim to be that and learn to prioritize that. The following is aimed to help us learn what a real friend is.

CIRCLES OF FRIENDSHIP

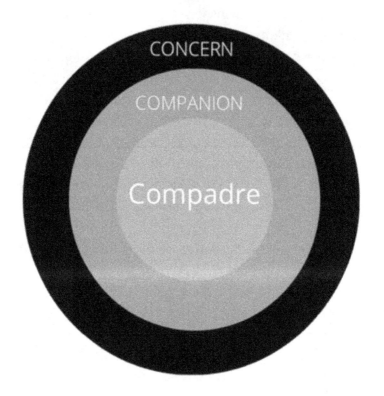

The three circles of relationships are important in helping us define the relationship. I get the three circles of friendship from the Bible.

> "A man of many companions may come to ruin, but there is a friend who sticks closer than a brother" (Proverbs 18:24 — ESV)

The three circles represent the three types of relationships you have. Have you ever heard of DTR? It stands for define the relationship. It's used mostly in dating, but I believe it's helpful in friendship as well. You cannot be friends with everyone. You can be friendly with everyone, but that's different than being a friend. As a Christian, we are called to love everyone, but that does not mean we grant everyone the same degree of access to us. Jesus had twelve disciples, and out of those twelve, He picked three to be in His inner circle. Jesus loved all the disciples, but for some reason He

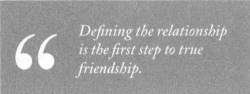

Defining the relationship is the first step to true friendship.

picked three to share more intimate parts of His life. The truth is, not everyone can handle direct access to you. That doesn't mean we aren't friendly with people who are not in our inner circle. It does mean that we gauge what we share and how we respond to people based on their level of friendship with us.

Defining the relationship is the first step to true friendship. Most friendships do not start by taking applications. Imagine a lemonade type stand for friendship. You take applications and only accept people who meet your qualifications. I don't know anyone who has done that. Most of us start friendships because of proximity. We are near someone; we need friends, so we develop a relationship. The friendship may have started because you went to school together, shared a hobby, lived in the same neighborhood, or because you work together. Because we are in close proximity to the person, we develop a relationship. Through the relationship, we learn what type of friend the person is. This can lead to hurt. When we quickly label someone a friend before we know if he or she possess the qualities of friendship, we open ourselves to hurt. In order to manage our expectations and help learn how to effectively respond to

each person, we need to DTR. In the three circles of relationships, the first circle is the compadre circle.

THE ONE ABOUT FRIENDS

The Scripture teaches that there is a friend who sticks closer
than a brother. Meaning, there is a person who will stick by
your side through thick and thin. Nothing will show you who
your true friends are more than failure. When life is going great,
you can collect a group of people who want to be around you.
It's in difficult seasons that you see who are your true friends
are. This is why this circle is the smallest of the three. You will
most likely only have a few true friends. The size of the circle
also represents access to you. Those in the third circle have the
least access to you. Those in your compadre circle are your ride
or die friends. These are the ones that you share life with. As
mentioned earlier Jesus had three of these friends. Out of His
twelve disciples He chose three to be in His inner circle. Those
three men shared some experiences with Jesus that the other
disciples did not.

Ultimately, for Christians, we need to have Godly friends
in our life. This is so important; I've dedicated the next chapter
to it. For now, let's look at the other two circles of friendship.
The three circles of friendship will help guide you to define the
relationship.

CIRCLE OF COMPANIONSHIP

Not every person in your life is a friend. Think about your
friends in high school. When I was graduating from high school,
we all made a bunch of empty promises to one another. We

were going to stay in touch and, like Zach Morris in *Saved by the Bell*, we were going to be friends forever.[11]

However, as time went by, there were only a couple of people who I stayed in contact with from my graduating class. I'm still friendly with anyone from my class but I don't prioritize those relationships. Most of those relationships were based off of proximity. We were close because we saw each other regularly, but as soon as we didn't see each other regularly, the relationship fizzled.

People you work with may be in your life even more than a friend, but don't confuse the relationship. People in your church may not be true friends. People who you are friends with on Facebook may be more followers than friends. Not everyone in your life is a friend. Not every person you call a friend will be there if your world falls apart. Not everyone will be there on your darkest days. To help manage expectations, we have to understand that not everyone who is friendly towards us is a real friend. Companions would fall more in line with what the Greek Philosopher, Aristotle, called friends of utility. These are people who are in your life, but are not necessarily going to be there for you on your darkest days. You may be friendly with them, but it's based on proximity. It's based on a shared interest or a mutual benefit. It's okay to have these relationships. These are people to whom you are friendly, but as soon as you lose close proximity, the relationship changes.

Expectations are so powerful! Unmet expectations are disappointments waiting to happen. In relationships, we often put unrealistic expectations on people. We should not put

---

[11] I realize you have to be a fan of the 90's tv show Saved by the Bell to get this reference and I'm okay with that. I love that show!

friendship expectations on companions. At times the lines will be blurred, but we should be careful with this. A companion may show up to help you move, let you borrow something, or

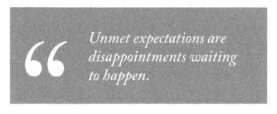

Unmet expectations are disappointments waiting to happen.

even come to a celebration like a birthday. Just don't get disappointed when a companion doesn't show up

like a friend would. The Bible says,

> "A man of many companions may come to ruin,
> but there is a friend who sticks closer than a
> brother" (Proverbs 18:24 — ESV).

A person with many companions may come to ruin. Having lots of people around you, doesn't mean you have lots of friends. Having lots of companions, doesn't mean you have quality friends. Having lots of companions isn't a bad thing, but we need to work hard to make sure we have some friends who stick closer than family.

Companions haven't earned the right to hear our deepest thoughts. Companions aren't the people with whom we go deep. Companions may cheer you on, but they aren't the ones who help you dig when you are in the trenches. To tell if a companion is ready to move to a friendship, you have to see if you can have tough conversations together. I believe we can disagree and still be friends, but that means that both people are willing to be friends. Some people aren't. We don't have to write them off completely. Instead, we should limit the access we give to them. We should manage our expectations by knowing they are more of a companion than a friend.

CIRCLE OF CONCERN

Some friends are not good influences. They are friends, but because of life choices, they shouldn't be in your inner circle. These would be friends of concern.

Jim Rohn famously said, "We are the average of the five people we spend the most time with." The Scriptures warn that we are not to be unevenly linked together. That is, we are to be careful with whom we align ourselves. At the exact same time, Christians are called to change the world. We cannot change the world if we avoid problematic people. The healthy way to do that is to think through your relationships. If someone is a negative influence, they need to be moved into your circle of concern.

CHARACTERISTICS OF FRIENDS OF CONCERN

1. If they don't give back to the relationship: A relationship takes two people. If one person is not working on the relationship or giving back to it then it's a concern.

2. If they are anti-Christianity: This doesn't mean that they have to be a Christian. Not everyone who isn't a Christian is anti Christianity. If you find someone doesn't respect your faith, then they should be moved to the circle of concern.

3. If they do not support your dreams/are negative about your dreams: This should be used with wisdom and caution. Most people lead with fear. You will have some friends who project their fear onto you. This doesn't mean that you cannot be friends with them. It does mean that you take their advice with a grain of salt.

4. They talk about people instead of to people. You can trust that if a friend talks to you about others, they will talk about you to others.

5. They tempt you to do things that do not honor Jesus. A great friend supports your standards and doesn't tempt you. If you have a friend who does not respect your convictions, then they should be moved to the circle of concern.

6. If a person refuses to have healthy conflicts: Conflict are a part of relationships. If a person unloads on you, refuses to talk about issues, or will not deal with unhealthy issues, they should be moved to the circle of concern.

Some people just love drama. Some people love conflict. Some people love to fight. This should be a major concern. As mentioned earlier, Scripture speaks to these types of people.

> Warn a divisive person once, and then warn them a second time. After that, have nothing to do with them. You may be sure that such people

are warped and sinful; they are self-condemned (Titus 3:10-11).

This doesn't mean that the relationship is over forever. It means that you cannot be in a healthy relationship with him or her until something changes. You may have to pray for the person from a distance. You may have to take a break from him or her. You may have to set up a boundary. Notice though, the first step to dealing with divisive people is to warn them. The second step is to warn them again. I believe you start with friendship and communicate the issue. Some people though just love to fight.

I heard a friend share a story about one of his divisive friends. When they were in college, they would go out on the weekends. Almost every weekend his friend would get into fights. Before they would leave, he would beg his friend to not get into a fight. His 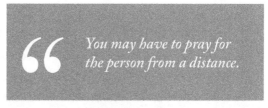 friend would assure him that he wouldn't fight, but every weekend the result was the same. He finally had a crucial conversation with his friend and asked him why he fights so much. His friend said, "To tell you the truth, I just love fighting." That's a friend that you should be concerned about. So how do you deal with a friend of concern?

You only hang out with friends of concern on your terms. For the example above, it would mean not going out with this friend who loves to fight on the weekends. As a parent, we try to monitor who our kids play with. It's easier to do when we invite them into our life. We want our kids to be leaders and to have influence. We also want to protect them as much as we can. We do that by inviting their friends into our life. We want our house to be the safe place for our kids and their friends. When it comes to relationships, we have to be honest with our limits. You should know what you can handle and what you can't. It takes being brutally honest with yourself. If a person in your life influences you to do anything that doesn't honor Jesus, then he or she should be moved to your circle of concern. You can still hang out with that person as long as it's on your terms. He or she may not accept this, and you have to be okay with that. I personally wouldn't advertise it or make a big deal about it. I simply would take the initiative and invite them to do things in which we both can equally benefit from the time together.

WHAT DOES THIS HAVE TO DO WITH OFFENSE

The circles of friendship should not be used to callously label people. They should be used to help navigate the different relationships we have, and thus manage our expectation. I am not as offended by a person who is in my circle of concern. I don't hold them to the same standards. I don't expect them to be life giving friends. This goes for strangers on the Internet. If someone throws shade at you, insults, or is critical of you, it will sting. To help it sting less, consider the source. Does this person know you? If not, then work hard at not letting this random person's opinion impact your day. You can bless and release. I can remain friendly to them because I'm managing my expectations. Unfortunately, there is a lot of negativity online. My family loves making fun videos on TikTok. We have had some success and had a view videos go viral. It's been my experience that whenever I have a video go viral on TikTok, the trolls come out of hiding. The vast majority of my videos are filled with positive comments. Once a video goes viral and starts reaching people that do not follow me, it becomes easy for strangers to attack. I see many people online address the haters and trolls by replying to them. It's been my experience that engaging with the trolls doesn't change their opinion. The reason is, they don't have a friendship with you to begin with. They are hiding behind their computers and cowardly attacking. It is not enjoyable, but I can promise you that I don't lose sleep over the haters. The reason is, they aren't my friends. They are strangers on the Internet. When I manage my expectations it helps me not get so easily offended.

Not everyone who will read this book is active on social media and that's okay. You will have people in your life that will offend you, and my challenge to you is to examine the source. Is the criticism from a friend? Is the criticism from someone who has your best interest in mind? There are some people in my area that don't like me. As a recovering people pleaser this is difficult for me to accept. I am able to bless and release them because they don't want a relationship with me. It is to exhausting trying to convince people who don't want to like me change their opinion. Instead, I want to continue living my life and pour into the people I do know. I aim to be so busy living for Jesus that I don't have time to convince others to like me.

The same goes for a companion. Companions can flake out and not show up when you need them. Companions can be great to have, but I don't expect them to be my ride or die friends. I want you to think about some of your relationships. Are you putting unrealistic expectations on companions? Do you have some friend of concern that you are allowing to pull you down? Who are your true friends and what makes them good friends? When we know all of this, it helps us manage our expectations. When we have the right expectations, we should be able to know what to do with our offense. When a person who I'm concerned about offends me, it should feel different than a friend. I expect people in my circle of concern to let me down. When a companion flakes on me, I'm less offended because my expectation changes. Remember Rabbi Weisser from chapter 1? It is easier to reach out and try to win someone over when you don't need them to be a true friend to you. Sure, we don't enjoy when people make fun of us or put us down, but when you consider the source it should change your expectation. Someone that is in your circle of concern becomes a person to influence and win over. Because they are in your circle of concern you should manage your expectations. They will probably let you down. They may not treat you with respect. They may be offensive, but you can still show them respect and love because you aren't counting on them to be a positive influence in your life. When a friend offends, it should feel different. Because they are a friend, I can lead with friendship. A friend is worth fighting for. A friend is worth engaging in hard conversations. A true friend will be there for you. In the next chapter, we are going to discuss Godly friends, but before that, here are some questions for discussion.

Questions:

1. Are you a person who makes friends easily or does it take some extra effort?

2. How does leading with friendship help you get less triggered?

3. Who are your ride or die friends?

4. How would you define a true friend?

5. Define your relationships by deciding who is a companion, friend of concern, and a true friend. This shouldn't be shared with a lot of people. It's an internal way to protect your expectations and ultimately your heart.

CHAPTER 14

COMPADRES

"And friends are friends forever if the Lord's the
Lord of them." – Michael W. Smith

In order to have great compadres, it is important to define
a friend. I've found one of the best examples of friendship
comes from the Old Testament of the Bible. David was the
shepherd boy who had just defeated the giant named Goliath.
After he kicks the giant's tail, he is brought before the king.
King Saul was the first king of Israel, and he plays a vital part
in David's life. He is not a great leader, and he does a lot of
wrong towards David. It's in this meeting with the king that
David meets a true friend, and that's where our text picks up:

> After David had finished talking with Saul,
> Jonathan became one in spirit with David,
> and he loved him as himself. From that day
> Saul kept David with him and did not let him
> return home to his family. And Jonathan made
> a covenant with David because he loved him
> as himself. Jonathan took off the robe he was
> wearing and gave it to David, along with his

tunic, and even his sword, his bow and his belt
(1 Samuel 18:1-4).

So, Jonathan made a commitment to David. It's a covenant. It's an oath. A covenant refers to two or more parties
bound together.

Covenants are so important to the Bible. Today we don't
deal with a lot of covenants. We do contracts. Contracts are necessary today. A contract is an agreement between two people,
and it helps spell out what each person will do. If one of the
people involved with a contract doesn't hold up part of the deal,
then you end the contract. That's not the way a covenant works.
A covenant is a promise. It's a pledge. It's a commitment that
goes beyond our circumstances. If you are familiar with the
Old Testament, then you may know about Noah's ark. God told
Noah to build an ark because He was going to save him from an
upcoming flood. Noah builds that ark and then the animals they
came by twosies twosies. After the flood, God made a covenant with Noah to never flood the entire earth again. Covenants
are all throughout the Bible. Because of Jesus, we have a new
covenant. The new covenant is that, through belief in Jesus, we
have unconditional love and access to God. So, when people
become Christians and put their faith in Jesus, they get this new
covenant. It's amazing. The covenant means that we are loved
by God. You may struggle to love yourself, but you can't shake
the love of God. Now, this is important. It's important because
so many of us don't have great friendships because we have
contract relationships instead of covenant relationships. Author
and researcher Simon Sinek says,

Millennials will admit that many of their relationships are superficial, they will admit that they don't count on their friends, they don't rely on their friends. They have fun with their friends, but they also know that their friends will cancel on them when something better comes along. Deep meaningful relationships are not there because they never practiced the skill set, and worse, they don't have the coping mechanisms to deal with stress. So when significant stress begins to show up in their lives, they're not turning to a person, they're turning to a device, they're turning to social media, they're turning to these things which offer temporary relief. – Simon Sinek

Now, Sinek is referring to Millennials, but I believe what he said contains a lot of truth for any age. The human race has moved from in person relationships to online relationships. As great as social media can be, it also has some negative effects. One of the side effects of social media is it gives us more companions, but not necessarily more real friends. So, when life falls apart, the so-called online friends may not be there for you. We also aren't learning to deal with our stress. Instead, we practice escaping our stress, and being online is an easy escape. Contrast that with real friendships. Friendships take work. Friendships take sacrifice and time. Friendships are incredibly important for everyone. For Christians, it is essential that we have Godly friendships. The question is, what is a Godly friend? This is important to define. If we do not define it, we may label a companion a friend when, in reality, they do not meet those requirements. Based on Jonathan and David's relationship, I believe there are four qualifications for Godly friendships. Let's look at them.

THE RECIPE FOR GODLY FRIENDSHIP

Godly Friendships

1. Require great commitment.

We don't have great friendships because we don't like to commit to people. As Christians, we believe that marriage is a covenant. That means it's a permanent relationship. So, if you are single and ready to mingle, please be so careful about who you date. Who you date could end up being someone you marry. You don't want to marry someone who is a project or who you think may have some potential. Marriage is amazing but it's tough.

> We don't have great friendships because we don't like to commit to people.

The Bible says, "Charm is deceptive, and beauty is fleeting; but a woman who fears the Lord is to be praised." Proverbs 31:30. My takeaway from that verse is there are not attractive people in the old folks home. There is nothing wrong with appreciating someone's beauty, but a marriage is a life long commitment that has to be built on something that won't change. Looks fade! This is why it's so important to marry someone with the same spiritual convictions as you. Every marriage will have some struggle, and it's faith in God and a covenant relationship that will keep a couple together!

When you marry someone, you need to know you are making a covenant. Through thick and thin, I'm committed to you. A covenant of marriage should cause a Christian to give his or her all towards their spouse. A covenant of marriage should lead us to work towards fixing problems. A covenant of marriage should cause us to give our best. What if we also had that type of commitment to a friend?

Godly friendships involve great commitment. It takes time and intentionality to have a great friendship. That doesn't mean that you will see a friend every day, but it does mean that there should be regularly scheduled time to be in each other's lives.

We want great friendships without great commitment. We want close friends simply because we exist. Friendship takes hard work. It's worth it, but make no mistake about it, it takes work.

JONATHAN IS THE REAL MVP

What we will see next in David's life is how Jonathan's covenant to David made a big difference in his life. Jonathan makes a commitment to David and then the poo hits the fan. Saul was the king and he was Cuckoo for Cocoa Puffs. He became jealous of David and tried to kill him. Look at the text:

> Saul told his son Jonathan and all the attendants to kill David. But Jonathan had taken a great liking to David and warned him, "My father Saul is looking for a chance to kill you. Be on your guard tomorrow morning; go into hiding

and stay there. I will go out and stand with my father in the field where you are. I'll speak to him about you and will tell you what I find out."

Jonathan spoke well of David to Saul his father and said to him,

"Let not the king do wrong to his servant David; he has not wronged you, and what he has done has benefited you greatly. He took his life in his hands when he killed the Philistine. The Lord won a great victory for all Israel, and you saw it and were glad. Why then would you do wrong to an innocent man like David by killing him for no reason?"

Saul listened to Jonathan and took this oath: "As surely as the Lord lives, David will not be put to death."

So Jonathan called David and told him the whole conversation. He brought him to Saul, and David was with Saul as before. (1 Samuel 19:1-7).

This takes us to the second thing that Godly friendships require.

Godly Friendships:

1. Require great commitment.

2. Require loyalty.

If you want to know who your loyal friends are, listen to how your friends talk about their other friends. If you have a friend who is constantly putting down other people or talking gossip about other people, I can guarantee you that they are also doing the same about you. Make a commitment today to not be a person that talks behind other people's backs. Talk to people instead of about people. If there is an issue address it with the person. If you do need to process a relationship commit to only talk to someone who can help you solve the issue. Talking to someone who can't help you restore the relationship is gossip and has no place in a Christian's life. Because Jonathan made a commitment with David, when King Saul, his dad, came to him and trashed David's name, Jonathan stayed loyal. He came to David's defense.

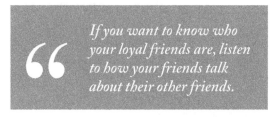

If you want to know who your loyal friends are, listen to how your friends talk about their other friends.

> So, Jonathan made a covenant with the house of David, saying, "May the Lord call David's enemies to account." And Jonathan had David reaffirm his oath out of love for him, because he loved him as he loved himself (1 Samuel 20:16-17).

Great friends are based around an oath, a covenant, a commitment that says, I'll be loyal to you. That takes us to the third quality of a Godly friendship.

SACRIFICE TO GET WHAT IS MOST IMPORTANT

Godly Friendships

1. Require great commitment.

2. Require loyalty.

3. Require sacrificial love.

Notice that Jonathan reaffirmed his commitment to David and he shows that he loved him as he loved himself. True love involves some form of sacrifice. It is not love if it doesn't cost you something. Great relationships happen intentionally, not accidentally. That means that if you want a great friendship, you must prioritize and carve out some time together. It may not be weekly, but it should be on a consistent basis. You may not have the time to go on vacation with your friends, but you have an hour a month to do something fun with them. It's not a real friendship if you aren't willing to sacrifice something. Jesus is the best illustration of this, in that, Jesus loved us so much He willingly sacrificed His life for us.

A mistake I see a lot of people make is prioritizing money, houses, and stuff over friendships. When buying a house, taking a job, picking a church, or making any life decision, does friendship filter into your decision-making process? Unfortunately, I see people make decisions all the time that end up negatively impacting great friendships. We act as if friends grow on trees and can be found anywhere. I've moved enough to know that we are not guaranteed to find great friendships and community. I'm not saying you should always put your friends before your career, buying your dream house, or moving, but I would argue that friendship should be a part of the decision process.

People can be messy. Relationships take work. It can be appealing to think about moving away from people. But think about it this way, in the prison system what is the punishment for inmates who misbehave? Solitary confinement. The reason is, too much alone time is a punishment. We aren't the best versions of ourselves when we are left alone. The Scripture is clear that God wired us to need one another.

> "Whoever isolates himself seeks his own desire;
> he breaks out against all sound judgment"
> (Proverbs 18:1— ESV).

When we are in isolation, we don't make the best choices. The spiritual enemy knows that we are stronger in community. It's when we are isolated that he often attempts to mess with us. When we are alone and don't think anyone will find out, we make poor choices. When we are isolated and unmotivated, we make the choice to not be our best selves. Isolated, we tend to break out against all sound judgment. It's not how God has wired us.

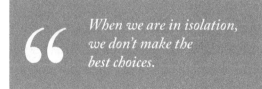

When we are in isolation, we don't make the best choices.

We isolate because it's easier. It's easier to make decisions without taking anyone else into account. It's easier to do what we want than to compromise for the good of a relationship. Isolation is easier, but it's deadly. Think about it, Jesus had twelve friends with whom He surrounded Himself. In fact it has been often joked about that the greatest miracle of Jesus' life was having twelve friends as a thirty year old adult. Out of that twelve, He had three who were in His inner circle. The Savior of the world, who had a one-on-one relationship with God, prioritized relationships! How much more do you and I need friendships? It is a sacrifice to have friends, but it's so worth it!

This is one of the main reasons I prioritize small groups at church. It is a weekly date that ensures I get to see friends. When life gets busy, we can put friendship on a back burner. Being in a group is one way that ensures I prioritize friends, even when life is busy. This is why I don't take a break from small groups. I believe they are that important!

LET'S KEEP READING

Let's keep reading our text to get to the fourth requirement of a Godly friendship. The text says,

> Jonathan said to David, "Go in peace, for we have sworn friendship with each other in the name of the Lord, saying, 'The Lord is witness between you and me, and between your descendants and my descendants forever.'" Then David left, and Jonathan went back to the town (1 Samuel 20:42).

This may seem self-explanatory but it's so important...

Godly Friendships

1. Require great commitment.

2. Require loyalty.

3. Require sacrificial love.

4. Require God.

Notice their friendship was a covenant in the Lord. It's like what the great theologian Michael W. Smith says, "And friends are friends forever if the Lord's the Lord of them." If you were a Christian in the 90s and didn't listen to Michael W. Smith, did you even experience Jesus? I kid, I kid.

If you want to grow in your relationship with God, then get you some Godly friends. I know that phrase is not grammatically correct, but that's what I'm challenging you to do. Go get some Godly friends! This might mean that you have to limit time with ungodly friends. Remember the circle of concern? I'm not implying that you should never hang out with people in your circle of concern. In order to influence them, you need to spend some time with them. What I am advocating for is for you to be careful. Pray for them, and at the same time watch their influence in your life. You should have some ungodly friends because you want to be a good example to them, but at the same time you should not allow them to influence you.

Now, this is crucial because I'm convinced that when two people commit to Godly friendships, they will have a lot less offense between them. For one, a true friend is one with whom we are willing to have hard conversations. For another thing, it helps us not hold companions to the same standards we would a friend. Life is tough, and we desperately need likeminded people who will be there for us during tough times. We need to have great friends that we can be there for during difficult times. When we understand the circles of friendship, we can manage our expectations while still holding on to the friendship. If a

Godly friend ever becomes a person who doesn't follow after God, we don't have to end the relationship. We have to redefine the relationship. They move to the circle of concern. I am convinced that when we have covenant friendships, everyone involved will be less tempted to walk away from the faith. These friendships are worthy of sacrifice.

A covenant friendship means we will commit to the friendship over the offense. It means we will have a difficult conversation when offense happens. It means we won't run at the first sign of difficulty. Friendships are worth fighting for. They are not easy to develop, but they are worth the effort!

One final note before we leave this chapter. There have been multiple occasions where I did not have a great godly friend in my every day life. In those cases I have prayed and God provided. I believe this is a prayer God honors. Relationships are so important! God created us to need others so I believe he will help us find godly friendships. If you don't have a godly friend pray and ask God to bring you one. In the meantime make sure that you are being the type of friend you want to have. Don't wait to be a faithful, loving, godly friend until you have one. Start being the type of friend you want and pray that God will bring a true friend to you.

Questions:

1. Out of the four requirements for Godly friendship, which one comes easiest to you?

2. Out of the four requirements for Godly friendship which one is the most challenging for you?

3. How can defining the relationship be helpful in helping us do something productive with our offense?

4. Who is your closest friend? Is it a Godly relationship? Why or why not?

PART IV

We naturally think about ourselves. We put our needs ahead of others. We see world events through our own personal lens and wonder, "How does this affect me." We are selfish creatures by nature. So, when it comes to offense, it's natural to think about oneself. A mistake I see so many Christians make is putting the offense over the relationship. You will get offended, but what you do with that offense is up to you. In this final section, my goal is to inspire and influence you to become a hospitable Christian, so that you will put relationships ahead of offense.

CHAPTER 15

IT'S HARD TO BE OFFENDED WHEN YOU PRACTICE HOSPITALITY

"Hospitality means primarily the creation of free
space where the stranger can enter and become
a friend instead of an enemy." –Henri Nouwin

B eing offended blinds us to our own actions. Because offense is a hurt, we demand justice for what offends us, but then at the same time we desire grace for the times when we offend others. We demand justice for our hurt, but request grace for the hurt we cause.

Do you remember Cecil the lion? A few years ago, a dentist from America went to Africa, tracked and then killed a protected lion named Cecil. When news of this broke, the Internet went berserk. The lion was being studied and was supposed to be protected. This dentist was in the wrong. As I was reading an article on this event, I decided to go to the comment section of the article. The comments are a perfect example of how we demand justice when we are hurt. The following shows how offense blinds us and makes us inconsistent. The comments consistently said, "We should kill the dentist." Or "I hope the dentist gets shot." Those who were offended by the dentist shooting a lion were the same ones who suggested the dentist should be killed. That makes zero sense. Neither do we when we get offended. We get offended and go off the deep end. Our offense blinds us from rational thinking. Piggy backing off the Cecil the lion incident, another outrage erupted on the Internet. This time, it was from a photo that movie director, Steven Spielberg, posted. The image he posted was on the set of the movie *Jurassic Park*. I so wish I had permission to share the photo in this book. It's worth a quick Google search. Spielberg was in front of a fake triceratops on the film set of the first Jurassic Park movie. The fake triceratops was lying down sick. The picture caused some outrage. Once again, I went to the comment section. My favorite comment was, "Despicable photo of a recreational hunter happily posing next to an animal he just slaughtered. Please share so the world can name and shame this man!" IT WAS A FAKE DINOSAUR!

Being offended blinds you to your own actions. You won't care how you come across or if you are in the wrong. All you will be able to see is the hurt the other person caused you. In this scenario, the outrage was over something that wasn't even

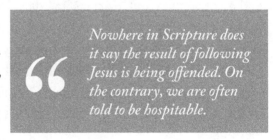

Nowhere in Scripture does it say the result of following Jesus is being offended. On the contrary, we are often told to be hospitable.

real. It wasn't a poached animal. IT WAS A FAKE DINOSAUR! Those jokers have been extinct for a minute. Offense is so blinding, it causes us to be blind to our own reactions.

HOSPITALITY TO THE RESCUE

Influence and friendship are two powerful tools to help us fight against being offended. A third tool we need to put in our toolbox is hospitality. We naturally think about ourselves, so when we intentionally show hospitality, we will become less offended.

Nowhere in Scripture does it say the result of following Jesus is being offended. On the contrary, we are often told to be hospitable. Here's one example:

> "Above all, love each other deeply, because love
> covers over a multitude of sins. Offer hospitality
> to one another without grumbling" (1 Peter 4:8-9).

In order to get the most out of this text, we need a little context for this verse. What would you say if the Democratic Party held a convention and, on the same day, the Republican Party held a convention at the exact same building. I'm not asking for your politics. I am simply asking for your initial reaction to these two groups holding a meeting in the exact same room. What words come to your mind when you think of this scenario? Probably words like "crazy," "chaotic," "Civil War" come to your mind.

This scenario is what we call church. Church is different backgrounds, races, and political leanings all in the same room. It's true today, and it was true in Peter's day. The author of the verse you just read was one of Jesus' best friends. In his day, Christianity was just starting and was made up of two groups of people. You had Jewish Christians, and you had Gentile Christians.

The Jewish Christians and the Gentile Christians got along about the same way as Republicans and Democrats. This would be a very difficult church to lead.

The Jewish Christians were offended by the Gentile Christians because the Gentile Christians didn't practice all the Jewish customs. The Gentile Christians were offended by the Jewish Christians because they felt they were legalistic and kept cramming old religious practices down their throats. To make matters worse, Christians were often persecuted by the Roman government. In the midst of all of this turmoil the writers of the New Testament continually told Christians to unite. We must be unified if we are going to change the world. Keep that in mind when we read Peter's words to Christians:

> "Above all, love each other deeply, because love
> covers over a multitude of sins" (1 Peter 4:8).

"Above all" means this is the ultimate calling in life. Love each other deeply. Why? "Because love covers over a multitude of sins." Our culture teaches that, in order to love people, you must agree with them. Scripture teaches that when we love those with whom we disagree, it covers over a multitude of sins. Christians aren't called to agree with everyone; we are called to love everyone. Love doesn't mean that we water down what we believe. It doesn't mean that we change the meaning of Scripture to make

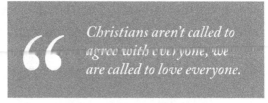

Christians aren't called to agree with everyone, we are called to love everyone.

people feel more comfortable. Like Jesus, we can still call sin (sin), and love those who disagree. Peter was writing to people who fundamentally disagreed with one another. Jews and Gentiles didn't see eye to eye. Peter didn't tell them to agree; he told them to love. There are certain things that people believe that are so offensive to us, we can't imagine being in relationship with them. To that, Peter says to love deeply because the love of Jesus covers over a multitude of sins. Right after Peter tells us to love deeply, he gives a command about hospitality. Look at what Peter says next:

> "Offer hospitality to one another without grumbling" (1 Peter 4:9).

So, the way we show love to one another is to offer hospitality. Remember this was written to Jews and Gentiles who fundamentally disagreed with one another. It's difficult to influence people with whom we are not in relationship. It's difficult to show love to those with whom we disagree if we aren't in close proximity to them. Peter challenged Christians to do more than just tolerate one another. He challenges us to offer hospitality to those with whom we disagree. This type of hospitality would change the world. We are so addicted to being right that offering hospitality to those with whom we disagree seems impossible. Maybe that's why Peter says to offer hospitality without grumbling. It's as if he knew the Jews and Gentiles in the church wouldn't want to show hospitality to each other. To truly show someone love, we must learn to show hospitality without grumbling.

HOSPITALITY IS A CHOICE

Research shows that whenever humans feel forced to do anything our motivation plummets.

The law of psychological reactance says, "If someone tells you to do something, you probably won't feel like doing it, even if you had otherwise wanted to."

If you have kids, you can relate to the law of psychological reactance. When a kid feels they are forced to do something, they become terrorists. You do too. Here is something that helps fix one's attitude. Whenever you feel like you have to do something and you really don't want to change your attitude just tell yourself, "I don't have to; I get to." Have you ever felt forced to offer hospitality. Have you ever had a thought like, "I don't want my mother-in-law to stay with us, but I don't have a choice." There is a d i f f e r e n c e

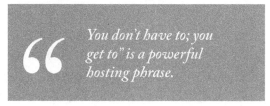

You don't have to; you get to" is a powerful hosting phrase.

between hosting or putting up with someone. Hospitality, without grumbling, means we have to choose to serve others and have a good attitude doing it. That might mean, you have to change your perception. You don't have to host your mother-in-law; you get to.

"You don't have to; you get to" is a powerful hosting phrase. Try saying it next time you feel forced to do something you don't want to do. I say this often while putting away laundry. I don't mind putting away laundry, but there are times when a pile of clean clothing has been placed on my bed. I don't see said laundry until I'm ready to go to sleep. In that moment, I'm not happy to do laundry, but each piece of clothing represents someone I love. I won't always get a chance to put away laundry for the people I love. Saying out loud, "I don't have to do this, I get to," focuses my brain on what is really important…the people I love. It can also happen for you. One day, you may miss folding clothes for someone who is no longer around. It's not just laundry. It's anything that we do for others. We don't always feel like showing hospitality, but we should choose to do it anyway. We don't have to, but we get to. We get to serve people we love. This phrase truly changes a perspective and, thus, can change a mood.

You don't have to be hospitable; you get to. You don't have to be welcoming to others; you get to. You and I get to do this because we represent Jesus. That is an honor!

IT'S ALL GREEK TO ME

When Peter wrote this letter to Christians, he wrote it in the Greek. The word he uses is Pheloxenos – means showing love to strangers. Peter is saying that, as Christians, we are to love one another deeply, and at the same time, we are to love strangers.

If, as Christians, we don't love each other, well then, why would anyone want to join us? And if we don't love others, well then, why would they want to join us. Peter gives us a command to be a certain kind of person, namely, the kind that doesn't resent having to be hospitable.

DIRTY ROTTEN SPACESHIPS

Think about this. When we host others, it causes us to take our eyes off ourselves. Hosting is a lot of work. It's why more people don't do it. But when we don't do it, we have a tendency to only think about ourselves. It's like this.

Have you ever watched a space shuttle launch? The physical force of gravity pulls everything to the center of the earth. In order to break free from earth-centered life, thousands and thousands of pounds of energy have to push the space shuttle away from the center. Just like gravity pulls things down, there is also a psychological force of gravity that constantly pulls our thoughts and affections and physical actions inward toward the center of our own selves and our own homes.

Therefore, the most natural thing in the world is to neglect hospitality. It is the path of least resistance. All we have to do is yield to the natural gravity of our self-centered life, and the result will be a life so full of self that there is no room for hospitality. We will forget about it, and we will neglect it. So, the Bible bluntly says, "Stop that!" Build a launching pad. Fill up your boosters. Blast out of your self-oriented routine. Stop neglecting hospitality. Practice hospitality!

Think about it. When you get offended, it's all you can see. You don't see how your actions are going to impact others. You don't see how you could be in the wrong. Being offended blinds us to our own actions.

What if you just started your day every day saying, "I am going to choose to be hospitable." Why? Because it's hard to be offended when I'm practicing hospitality. Christians should be the most loving and hospitable people around.

MORE SCRIPTURE

The idea of hospitality is a theme all throughout Scripture. I love what the Apostle Paul says about this. Some think that Paul's writing on this actually influenced what we read from Peter. Look at what Paul says:

> Be joyful in hope, patient in affliction, faithful in prayer. Share with the Lord's people who are in need. Practice hospitality (Romans 12:12-13).

Being offended is natural. Being hospitable to those we don't agree with is not natural. That's why we have to practice it. How do we practice it? We practice it in every relationship we have. We should practice hospitality with our family. We should practice hospitality with our friends. We should get so good at practicing hospitality that it becomes natural to us.

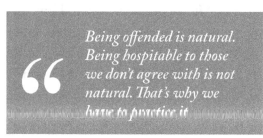

Hospitality changes the way you see others. When you are hospitable, you say things like, "Can I get you something?" "What would you like to do?" When our kids have guests, we say things like, "Make sure you ask what they want to do." Sometimes, my kids don't want to do what their guests want to do. When that happens, we say, "You get to do what you want often. Because they are our guest, I need you to do what they want to do."

Being a good host, gets your attention off of yourself. Therefore, you will become less easily offended. I'm convinced if Christians would practice hosting, it would change the way they interact with people. At the beginning of this chapter, I shared how offense blinds us to our own actions. If offense blinds us, being hospitable gives us our sight back. Practicing hospitality causes us to see past our hurt. Practicing hospitality helps us take the attention off ourselves. Practicing hospitality helps tear down barriers and gives Christians the platform to change the world.

A STORY ABOUT HOSPITALITY

Back in 2013, the director of Campus Pride led a boycott against Chick-fil-A. Shane Windmyer started Campus Pride, and it has become the largest organization for the LGBTQ community. He was offended by some of the organizations Chick-fil-A supports and by Dan Cathy's public support of the traditional view of marriage. During the boycott, he received a surprising phone call by Dan Cathy, the owner of Chick-fil-A. At first, he was nervous because he had just led a nationwide boycott of Chick-fil-A. He sheepishly took the call, and it lasted an hour. From there, they continued to talk on a regular basis. This fact alone would shock both Shane and Dan's audiences.

What happened next shocked everyone, and it's an amazing picture of Christian hospitality.

Throughout the conversations, Shane felt that Dan expressed a sincere interest in his life. He showed he wanted to get to know him on a personal level. He wanted to know about where he grew up, his faith, his family, even his husband, Tommy. In return, Shane learned about Dan's wife and kids and gained an appreciation for his devout belief in Jesus Christ and his commitment to being "a follower of Christ" more than a "Christian." This is so crucial. In Shane's own words, "Dan expressed regret and genuine sadness when he heard of people being treated unkindly in the name of Chick-fil-a — but he offered no apologies for his genuine beliefs about marriage." That's how you love someone without agreeing with them.

Because of their relationship, Shane ended the boycott of Chick-fil-A. He wrote about his relationship in the *Huffington Post* and the article ended with something that caught my attention. Look at his words.

> In the end, it is not about eating (or eating a certain chicken sandwich). It is about sitting down at a table together and sharing our views as human beings, engaged in real, respectful, civil dialogue. Dan would probably call this act the biblical definition of hospitality. I would call it human decency.

Come on someone! That's amazing! That is the biblical definition of hospitality! Hospitality isn't glossing over important issues. Hospitality doesn't mean that we don't hold to our convictions. It does mean that we treat people with respect and dignity as much as we can. It's the very nature of serving people, and it's what Jesus did for us.

Questions:

1. Who is the most hospitable person you know?

2. How can showing hospitality help us do something productive with our offense?

3. How does being a good host get our mind off of our offense?

4. What is one thing you can do to improve your hospitality?

CHAPTER 16

AM I THE HOST OR GUEST?

"True hospitality consists of giving the best of yourself to your guests."- Eleanor Roosevelt

As Christians we should learn to be amazing hosts. But what happens if we aren't the host? We aren't always in a position to host and that means sometimes we are the guest. I believe changing how we view ourselves will help us know how to navigate life's relationships.

Hosts and Guests

The difference between hosts and guests seems obvious, but it's important to think through this.

Hosts

Set the rules
Decide who is invited
Take the initiative to ensure everyone is comfortable
Assume ownership over the environment
Intentionally plan the events

Compare that to a guest...

Guests

Often bring a gift to offer appreciation to host
Try to follow the host's guidelines or rules
Display their best behavior
Respect that it is not their environment
Show up, but are usually not involved with the planning
of the event

As the host, you get to decide what you require from guests. Restaurants do this. Have you ever seen a sign on a restaurant door that says, "No shirt, no shoes, no service." So as the host, I can decide what I will allow and what I won't allow. On your social media account, you get to decide what to post and how others can engage with that. As the guest, I don't get to decide what is allowed, but I do get to decide if I want to stay or not.

When online, you get to decide if you are a host or a guest. Is it your Facebook page, your Instagram

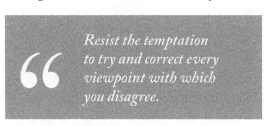

Resist the temptation to try and correct every viewpoint with which you disagree.

post, your blog, or your thought? If so, you can decide what you will allow. If someone is ugly in the comments, you can communicate with them that you don't allow that on your page. If you are the guest, you don't get to decide the content. You get to decide if you want to engage with it or not. Take Facebook for example. If you see a post that you disagree with, you get to decide what type of guest you want to be. You do not have to engage with the post. For example, I've never been to Hooters. Hooters exists in my area, but just because it's there, I don't have to visit. If someone else goes there, I don't have to share my opinion. There are lots of restaurants around.

Resist the temptation to try and correct every viewpoint with which you disagree. That's exhausting. If you are truly friends (see chapter 12) then you get to decide what type of guest you want to be on their post. Going back to the restaurant illustration, there really are bad guests. There are people who create a mess, tip poorly, and are exhausting to serve. As a Christian we should aim to be amazing guests. So, if you engage with a friend you disagree with, remember that it's their page or post. Remember to start with friendship.

You get to choose what type of guest or host you want to be.

This is an important thing to differentiate. You don't own Facebook. Therefore, when you see someone else's post, you are not in charge of it. If someone else posts something you don't like, you can decide if you are going to engage with it.

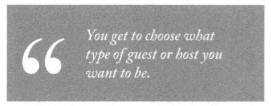

You get to choose what type of guest or host you want to be.

When you are a guest, don't hold other hosts to your standards. Be a good guest. As a Christian, you represent Jesus. That's important to remember. When someone you know posts an opinion that you fundamentally oppose, you don't have to reply to it.

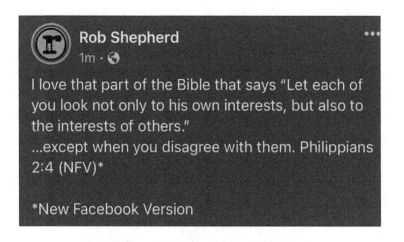

STICK WITH ME ON THIS

So often we look at those who are different and demand that they live according to our standards. We become triggered when those who vote differently have different opinions. We become triggered when another religion has a different view. We can become triggered when someone has a different opinion than ours. I don't believe a Republican can fix the Democrat party, and vice versus. We need Republicans to work hard and become the best they can at leading their party. We need Democrats to work hard at becoming the best leaders they can be. Both parties have issues that can only be fixed from within. It's easy to ignore your problems when you are hyper focused on the other side. I see this same kind of thing in the church world. Someone sees a pastor share a thought they disagree with, and they destroy him online. I don't think that rant changes anyone. It only gathers people who already agree and pushes away those who don't. It also comes across as holier than thou. Every group has its own issues. I believe we focus on other people's issues because we don't have to work on our own issues as long as we are hyper focused on someone else's. The problem is, our rants don't change the other person. I believe a more helpful approach is to stand for what you believe, and pray for those who disagree. Especially on social media, we should remember that we aren't always the host. We are the guest. As a guest, I get to choose if I want to stay or not. If I stay, I get to choose what type of guest I am going to be. Imagine walking into someone else's home and yelling at them for what they believe. If you wouldn't do that, I'm not sure why you would yell, argue, or engage negatively with someone online. It's the person's space, and they can post what they want. You get to choose whether you want to follow them, engage with them, or just scroll past. At the same time, think about what type of host you are. When you post on social media, you are a host. What type of host do you want to be? Imagine someone enters your house because you invite them; as soon as they walk in, you yell at them because they express an opinion that is different than yours? If you wouldn't yell at a guest in person, you shouldn't yell at them online.

Recognizing your role as a guest or a host helps with offense because it reminds us to take a second to pause and reflect. At times, our emotions get the best of us. We react to an infringement with a felony type anger. Remembering your role as a host or guest is so helpful...especially online.

SHOULD I ENGAGE?

Question: What do you do if you are hosting someone (whether in person or online) and they bring a mess into your space? For example, my family and I do not cuss. We don't shame others for cussing; it's their choice. However, when you hang out with me and I am hosting, I will respectfully ask you to not swear. This type of thing becomes trickier online. When you are hosting online and it is your post, it can become messy when other people get into the comments. The following will help you know when you should engage with someone you disagree with and how to still keep your influence.

When Should I Engage?

	Kind	Unkind
Listen	Engage	Cool off then engage
Not Listen	Bless & Release	Set a healthy boundary

The first step is to ask yourself if you can be kind. Remember, as both host and guest, you represent Jesus. If you cannot respond in kindness, then cool off until you can engage with kindness. You might have to write a letter that you never send, like Abraham Lincoln. If you can respond in kindness, then you ask a question about the person you are about to engage. Kindness doesn't mean you have to agree with the person. Kindness is not weakness. You don't have to lay down your opinion or ignore how you feel. If you want to make a difference you have to be different. Being kind takes great strength when disagreement is involved. This is how you can make sure you have some grace to the truth you want to share.

The second step is to reflect on whether the person you want to engage with is willing to listen or not. You may not know if they are willing to listen. If the relationship is strictly online, it becomes difficult to make that judgement. For a general rule of thumb — if the person is debating, sharing strong opinions, or argumentative, they probably aren't willing to listen.

Once you establish if you can be kind or unkind, you move down to decide if the person is willing to listen or not listen. If you can be kind, and the person is willing to listen, then you engage. If you can be kind, but the person is not willing to listen, then you bless and release. If you cannot be kind, but they are willing to listen, you cool off and make time to come back to engage in a respectful manner. If you cannot be kind and they are not willing to listen, you need a healthy boundary. The healthy boundary may be committing to pray for them and (at the same time) committing to not comment or read their posts. The boundary may be getting off social media for a spiritual fast. If what's online is controlling your behavior, you need a break.

WHAT DOES THIS LOOK LIKE IN REAL LIFE?

I've had to practice this, often. It is not always easy. Let me give you a real-life example. I've changed the names, but the content is the same.

During a season of lots of opinions and people being ugly online, I posted the following.

Rob Shepherd
Yesterday at 2:55am

"We must beware of a tyranny of opinion which tries to make only one side
of a question the one which may be heard. Ev
eryone is in favor of free speech. Hardly a day passes without its being
extolled, but some people's idea of it is that they are free to say what they
like, but if anyone says anything back, that is an outrage." – Winston
Churchill

Like · Comment · Share

👍 99 people like this.

↪ 56 shares

Joe Mama The Left controls every major institution in America. Mainstream
media, academia, administrative government, Hollywood, big tech. So if
"institutional racism" really does exist, whose fault would that be?
Like · Reply · 5 mins

Rob Shepherd Hey Joe Mama , I appreciate comments. Thanks for making
the time to comment. My post and the quote isn't in reference to institutional
racism. Help me connect the dots between the quote and your comment.
Like · Reply · 👍 12 · 1

Joe Mama Well it is the #1 subject that even pastors are now expected to
speak on. But most are only preaching against police brutality , racial
profiling. Preaching that yes black lives matter. But refusing to address the
evils of a lawless society, respect for authority and laws, BLM Marxist
foundation. They are only telling half the truth. How many pastors address
the effects of 75% of youths in USA Today are raised in fatherless homes.
Like · Reply · 👍 0 · 3

Rob Shepherd Joe Mama, thank you for making the time to explain.
Like · Reply · 👍 3 · 5

Write a comment ...

This is an example of bless and release. Joe Mama wasn't
interested in a conversation. He wasn't a Godly friend. I'm not
saying he is not Godly. I'm saying I don't know him. He was

a Facebook "friend" that I barely knew. That puts him in the circle of concern or the companion circle of friendship. Because I don't know him, it felt like he was looking to either sabotage my post or start an argument. I chose to not be offended by his comment, so I could be kind in my response. The next part was to find out if he was willing to listen. Based on his response and lack of questions to me, I made the judgment that he didn't want to discuss anything. I don't know him; he is not a friend. He doesn't want to listen, so therefore, I don't have to allow him to get me worked up. I can bless and release him. His opinion is not my problem to solve. Engaging him will only waste my time. That may seem strong, but if someone isn't willing to listen, then they aren't willing to change their opinion. After my response back to him, he dropped it. Now, if he came back and engaged again, I would have to have a crucial conversation with him and set up a healthy boundary. If he did this same type of thing on another post, I would address it because now there is a pattern. As a host, I want to make sure my guests know my expectations. He didn't come back, but if he had, I would have sent him a direct message and explained, "I enjoy dialogue and conversations online. I try not to be political, online. I understand you have some strong feelings. Please make sure that when you post on my page, comments stick to the subject at hand." If he refused to respect this boundary, there would be a consequence. A consequence may be hiding him on Facebook or unfriending him. Now, I personally would have a conversation before I would do that. Because of wanting to influence him, I would only unfollow as a last resort. I would only do that after I kindly shared my boundary, and he refused to accept it. Because of how I responded to his comment, I was able to end the conversation quickly.

You don't have to show up to every argument. Not every social media post is for you. It's okay for someone to have a different opinion. You don't have to correct everyone's wrong idea. You don't have to have an opinion on every hot button item! In fact, sometimes, it takes time to form a well thought out idea. Reacting to everything in the moment is premature birth for ideas. Remember, the

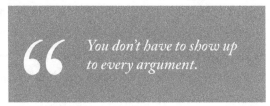

You don't have to show up to every argument.

goal is to do something positive with your offense. If you engage with rage, and it doesn't make a difference — what's the point? If you lose influence, then you won't be able to impact anyone. That is my whole point. As a good host, you get to decide what you allow into your space. However, as the host, you don't want to blast your guests every time you disagree with them.

> Jesus said, "Do not give dogs what is sacred; do not throw your pearls to pigs. If you do, they may trample them under their feet, and turn and tear you to pieces" (Matthew 7:6).

There is so much wisdom to this. We have to decide if someone can handle our pearls. There are some things worth fighting for. There are some things worth standing up against. But at the end of the day, we need to think about the big picture. If we railroad someone with our opinion, and it doesn't change them — what have we accomplished? If we argue and fight, but nothing good comes out of it — we are wasting our time. Can you be kind? That doesn't mean others will agree with what you say. It means that in your demeanor and tone you will show respect. Will they listen? That doesn't mean they will agree. Are they looking for a fight or are they trying to learn? If you can be kind, but they aren't willing to listen — then bless and release them. Going back to Paul in Athens, he was okay with the fact that he could only win some. We cannot win everyone. We can pray for our enemies. We can hope that by consistently living for Jesus and loving people well we can, over time, have influence over people. However, we have to accept the fact that we cannot change people. The goal is to determine who we can influence and release the energy and stress of not being able to influence everyone.

Here's a challenge for you. The next time you read a post online that causes you to feel angry, use the "When Should I Engage" chart to navigate how you should respond.

Questions:

1. When it comes to relationships, how does hosting help change how you interact with each person?

2. Do you have an example of showing kindness to someone when they didn't deserve it?

3. Look over the "When should I engage" chart. Which part of it is easiest for you? Which part is the most difficult?

4. Based on this chapter, what is your biggest takeaway?

5. Have you ever thought about being a host or guest in your daily interactions?

6. What would the Internet look like if all Christians were amazing hosts and guests?

CHAPTER 17

Hosts Ask Great Questions

"Asking questions is the first way to begin change." – Kubra Sait

I t doesn't take much for people to get offended. At times, it is as if people have a finger on the offense trigger and are just waiting to pull it. A number of times I've seen people over-react to something, but later come back and realize they had the wrong perception. It's easy to do. We aren't wired to believe the best. When someone doesn't meet our expectations, our brains will come to the conclusion that they did it on purpose. This is why when you don't text someone back, you know it's because you are busy. However, when someone doesn't text you back, your brain tells you it's because they now hate you and want nothing to do with you. At least, that's how my brain works.

So often the things we get worked up about simply need more information. Questions don't mean that we don't react. It means we ensure that we have the right information so we can react accordingly.

Remember, as a host, you should put your guests first. There's a reason why this is so hard to do. It's called Fundamental Attribution Error.

FUNDAMENTALLY FLAWED

Fundamental Attribution Error states: "When others wrong us, we assume the worst, but when we mess up it's for a good reason."

Here's how this looks.
When someone offends us, we say:
Why is he so lazy?
Maybe if she paid attention...
She did that on purpose!
He is so rude! It's just who he is.
There is something wrong with them!

Now, contrast that with what we do...

When I offend others, I say:
I was stuck in traffic.
I couldn't help it.
It's not my fault.
Why can't you show me some grace?

Now, please don't move past this too quickly. We can all benefit from this insight. We all love to assume the best about ourselves and the worst about others. We judge others by their behaviors and ourselves by our best intentions. Pastor Chris Hodges says it like this, "We've become great judges of others sins, but great lawyers of our own." Because an offense is a wound, we naturally react by assuming the worst about the other person. Fundamental Attribution Error tells us that this is how the human brain is wired. We are wired to assume the worst about others, but expect others to believe the best about us.

The next time you get offended, please do the hard work of finding out more information. Without additional information, your brain will tell you that the other person hurt you on purpose. Whenever there is an offense, there is a gap in the relationship. We need to choose what we are going to use to fill that gap. It's natural to fill the gap with negativity. In order to protect yourself from assuming the

The next time you get offended, please do the hard work of finding out more information.

worst, ask some questions. No one can see a motive. We can't read people's minds.

When we become offended, we assume the worst about the other person. The only reason they would have said that is because they are an idiot. The only reason they would have forgotten is because they are selfish. The only reason they would have done that is because they are evil. You see this a lot with media and the news. The news is presented like, the only reason millions of people vote differently than you is because they are fundamentally flawed. The other side is full of idiots; it's full of evil people who don't know what they are doing. That may be true, but if everyone who disagrees with you is an idiot — you have a pride issue.

This is where questions come in. When someone offends you, your brain will assume the worst. When you learn to ask great questions, it gives your brain time to calm down. In order to make the right decision, learn to ask questions.

Because offense blinds us to our own actions, we often react before we think. I think we've all had an overreaction and didn't realize it until later. My friend was once convinced that the rapture had occurred, but he was left behind. He returned to work after lunch, and no one was there. There was also an accident in front of his office, so the natural conclusion for a good Christian is that he's been left

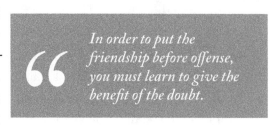

In order to put the friendship before offense, you must learn to give the benefit of the doubt.

behind. He wasn't left behind, but he's not alone in that type of conclusion. We quickly assess information and often come to wrong conclusions. So, before you react, ask questions.

An important skill that is essential in relationships is learning to ask questions. When you get offended, you may be tempted to turn a misdemeanor into a felony. You may be tempted to yell, boycott, or fuss at someone who doesn't meet your standards.

In order to put the friendship before offense, you must learn to give the benefit of the doubt. It's childish to assume that every time someone hurts your feelings, it is on purpose. Everyone in your life will offend you at some point. When offense happens, give the benefit of the doubt and learn to ask questions.

QUESTIONS TO BETTER UNDERSTAND

1. I know you care about me deeply. I'm missing some information. Can you help me understand why you said that?

2. I love our friendship! I'm feeling hurt, but I am sure I missed some information. Is there anything I should know?

3. I may be too sensitive about this topic. When I heard you say this I heard _____. Is that what you meant?

4. I'm feeling hurt, and I would love to feel connected again. You are a friend, so I want to make sure we have honesty. Did I do something to hurt you, or am I simply misunderstanding the situation?

The point is to lead with the friendship. That's what good hosts do! Your offense often will make you think the other person is an enemy. When we go in with offense, we often lead with defense. We attack. When our emotions are high, we have a difficult time hearing what the other person is saying. Have you ever had an argument that went nowhere because it just didn't seem like the other person understood what you were trying to say? The way that we can disagree and still be friends is when each person believes the best, and leads with friendship. We should strive to put people over opinions. We should strive to lead with friendship and believe the best.

Questions:

1. Is it easy or difficult for you to believe the best?

2. When have you come to the wrong conclusion because you didn't have all the information?

3. Questions are incredibly important in order to gain information. Look over the list of questions provided in this chapter. Which one do you think would be the most helpful for you? Write it out on a note card or put it in your phone so you have easy access to it. The next time your brain wants to believe the worst, pull out the question and remind yourself that you need more information.

4. How can asking questions help us not to turn those we disagree with into a villain?

EPILOGUE

I pray that everyone who reads this can be a beacon of light in an incredibly dark world. We may never get to a place of not being offended. We are too self-centered. We are all more fragile than we like to admit. We can't keep offense from knocking, but we can change our response to it.

We can each work at doing something productive with our offense. We can learn to let some things go. We can learn to address conflict in a healthy way. We can learn to turn an offense into a positive action.

I don't know if I've convinced you to change anything about how you respond to offense. I hope I have. You see, it's really difficult to shine when we don't look different than the world. People continually say, "Everyone is offended," so let's be different than everyone. The Apostle Paul said it this way...

> Do everything without grumbling or arguing,
> so that you may become blameless and pure,
> "children of God without fault in a warped and
> crooked generation." Then you will shine among
> them like stars in the sky (Philippians 2:14-15).

Christians shine when we "Do everything without grumbling or arguing." I know the verse doesn't say anything about being offended, but grumbling and arguing tend to be common responses to offense. What if instead of grumbling or arguing we prayed for the person that offended us? What if in that prayer we asked God for opportunities to show the person that offended us love? What if by showing them love we gained influence? What if by gaining influence we win them over to Christ? I don't know about you, but that sounds like shining bright to me.

In conclusion, I want to encourage you to live out what you've read in this book. Offense is everywhere, but we get to decide how we respond when it knocks. Respond with influence, friendship, and hospitality. Respond in a way that honors Christ and attempts to win the other side. Respond in a way that can turn an enemy into a friend.

Special Thanks

There are so many people that support me and specifically my writing. With this book there were a handful of people that spent extra time making sure this book was the best it could be.

To my mom, Marcia Shepherd, thank you for proofing this book multiple times. You saw this from a rough draft, to a title change, and a complete re-write. Your proofing for each stage was invaluable! Thank you for your time!

To my sister, Sarah Burggraf, thank you for making the time to read through the entire book, and give your editing suggestions. The book is better because of the time you spent with it, and I'm grateful!

Thank you to Jeff Mingee, Scott Rutter, Monica Shepherd, and Jacob Lambert for reading early versions of this book. I know it's not easy to offer constructive feedback, but you did. Because of your insight this book became a much better read!

Thank you Jason Covington for converting the images in this book. That was way over my pay grade and you did it with ease! I appreciate you!

Thank you Monica Shepherd for your support, opinions, time, and encouragement! It's not easy having a husband who invests money to write books that rarely make money. You have never made me feel bad for pursuing a writing career. Even more than that you have encouraged me to keep dreaming big! I love you with all my heart!

Thank you Next Level Church for loving Jesus, loving people, and making a difference! Even if I wasn't your pastor I'd love going to this church! It's so much fun, and we are truly changing the world together!

Thank you Jesus for using a broken person for your glory! My ultimate goal with writing is to help people know you and experience your love. I ask that you use the words in the book to do immeasurably more than I could ask or imagine.

OTHER BOOKS BY ROB SHEPHERD

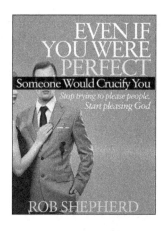

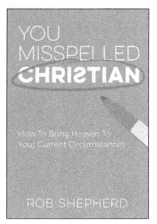

CONNECT
WITH ROB

Facebook: Rob Shepherd

Instagram: rob_shep

TikTok: robshep

Website: robshep.com

NEXT LEVEL
CHURCH

Love Jesus
Love People
Make A Difference

Nextlevelchurch.net
You Tube: nextlevelchurch757
Instagram: nextlevelchurch757

LEADING A CHURCH IS HARD.
WE MAKE IT EASIER.

Church BOOM's team of successful, seasoned, pastors want to help you face and overcome the obstacles keeping you from experiencing explosive growth in your church.

- Personal coaching call opportunities
- Video training modules
- Full library of downloadable resources
- Complete sermon series branding packages.

Learn more at:

CHURCHBOOM.ORG

LYVUX Information can be obtained
at www.ICGtesting.com
Printed in the USA
BVHW032008160323
660607BV00003B/5